Empowered Butterfly Method

Written By
Dr. Patricia Kaine MD - Speaker,
Author, and Retired Physician, Ohio,
USA
Simone Moir - Speaker, Author,
Holistic Practitioner, Glasgow,
UK - Scotland

Terms and Conditions

LEGAL NOTICE

"It's possible to go from distress to hope with a few simple sequential steps."
Patricia Kaine MD

"If your happiness depends on externals, you're in danger of mental health challenges."
Simone Moir

Forward

Just saying the word "suicide" can make one cringe. On the other hand, it can become an ever-present option that haunts and even provides a certain degree of solace. The pain involved can shake you to your core, wear you down, and cause you to question everything and anyone you value, including yourself. And yet, as a psychiatrist of thirty years, many have admitted to me that I was the first to ever ask and the first time they have ever uttered the words, "I have frequent thoughts of killing myself."

Patricia Kaine is a service-minded physician who reached out to me many years ago with a severe medical condition and an even more severe life-long depression. Despite and maybe because of her difficult upbringing, she brought her deep compassion and understanding to everyone she served. Given the depth and duration of her pain, I felt we were in for a war to even keep her alive.

But that's not what happened.

She knew the life path that thoughts of suicide could create, as several members of her family had taken their own lives. She saw the crushing effects of suicide on remaining family members and how this affected children, even herself. She endured the family secrets and the cardinal rule to tell no one.

But she knew better.

Sometime in her young life, she found her strength through serving others. As a doctor, she knew she was not alone in her frequent thoughts of suicide, although it often felt that way. She brought her thoughts and faith to each session and reached out for the tools she hoped God would provide. She embraced the term neuroplasticity, the fact that we can literally change the way our brain is wired. She took to heart that when we give our brain the opportunity to think and feel differently, we can create new neurons. She was intelligent and tenacious and learned the value of practice as she slowly forced her brain to form new neural pathways.

She not only survived but now thrives and is on her sustaining mission of hope and resolve to get the message out, "Suicidal ideations are common, and you can train your mind to think differently."

Her success leaves clues. There is an organic feel to what she shares. Her personal stories make sense and hold value. She knows what works and doesn't sugarcoat the effort it will take to gain ground and win. She shares wisdom regarding where best to apply efforts and when to rest. Most of all, she knows that thinking about suicide is real. There is no simple "getting over it," but there is a way to successfully put these thoughts to rest.

If you or someone you know struggles with suicidal ideation, take this book seriously. She calls the transformation of old destructive thoughts to a new way of living "The *Empowered Butterfly Method*." Add each aspect of her method to the one daily routine we all share, flushing our waste in our bathroom several times a day.

Michael L Seng, MD
Founder of **A Starting Point**
Retired Psychiatrist

Table of Contents

Empowered Butterfly Method............................ 1

Terms and Conditions 2

Forward 1

Table of Contents 5

Orientation... 13

What is The Empowered Butterfly Method?.................. 17

Why We Wrote This Book.............................. 19

Why You Should Read The 'Empowered Butterfly Method' 27

   Stats and Figures 29

How To Get The Most Out Of The Method: 33

   The stages of the *Empowered Butterfly Method* in 3 Sections... 38

Summary QUICK OVERVIEW 40

The Butterfly Method 43

Deep Dive.. 43

Section 1 The Caterpillar................................ 43

Chapter 1 45

E - Stands for Exit 46

   Let's take it deeper: 46

   What is it? 46

   How to do it?... 47

   Why does it work? 49

Thought-Stopping Techniques 49

Why is it included? 49

Example 50

Patricia's Story Police Whistle 50

Thought-Stopping Techniques 51

Research links and Further reading 53

Chapter 2 55

The M in empowered stands for Move 56

Let's dive deeper 56

What it is 56

How to do it: 57

Explore this practice to gain a deeper understanding:. 58

One at a time: 58

Our Inhale: 58

Notice: 59

On the Exhale: 60

CAUTION: 60

Our Pause: 60

What happens: 62

Example 64

Simone's Experience 64

Why it works 65

Why it is included 66

Questions that might come up in Chapter 2: 67

Research Links and Further Reading............................ 67

Chapter 3 69

'P' in empowered stands for pivot. 70

What it is 70

How to do it?... 71

Why it works 71

Why is it included?.. 72

Example - Story 73

Patricia's Experience 73

Questions that might come up in Chapter 3: 74

Research Links And Further Reading 75

The Butterfly Method 77

Section 2 - The Cocoon 77

Chapter 4 79

The 'O' in empowered stands for on and off. 80

Let's dive deeper... 80

What is it? 81

How to do it?... 82

Start:... 84

OPTIONAL:... 86

Why it works? 86

Why is it included?.. 87

Example - Story 88

Patricia's Experience 88

Questions that might come up in Chapter 4: 89

Research links and Further reading 90

Chapter 5 91

W in empowerment stands for Way Out......................... 92

What is it? 92

How to do it?.. 93

Why does it work? 94

Why is it included?.. 94

Example - story 95

Patricia's Experience 95

Questions that might come up in Chapter 5: 96

Research and Further Reading....................... 97

Chapter 6 99

The 2nd E in empowered stands for Envision 100

Let's go deeper... 100

What is it? 100

How to do it?.. 101

Consider these features:............................... 102

Why does it work? 102

Why does it work? 103

Why is it included?...................................... 104

Example.. 105

Patricia's Story 105

Questions that might come up in Chapter 6: 106

References and Further Reading 107

Chapter 7 109

R- stands for release, to get rid of completely 110

What is it? 110

Why does it work? 111

Why is it included? 112

Example - Story 114

Patricia's Story 114

Questions that might come up in Chapter 7: 116

References And Reading List 116

Chapter 8 119

The final E in empowered stands for END ALL 120

Let's go deeper 120

What is it? 120

How to do it? 121

Why does it work? 122

Why it is included 124

Example - Story 125

Simone's Experience 125

Questions that might come up in Chapter 8 126

References and Further Reading 127

The Butterfly Method 129

Section 3 - The Butterfly 129

Chapter 9 131

D in empowered stands for Do the new 132

Let's go deeper.. 132

What is it? 133

How it works: 133

Why does it work? 134

Why is it included?...................................... 135

Example - Story 136

Simone's Experience 136

Questions that might come up in Chapter 9............... 137

References and Further Reading 138

Sharing with communities   129

Practical steps into opening conversations in your community 139

Practical steps into opening conversations 141

Know the limits of The Empowered Butterfly Method when you advocate it:................................ 149

The full spectrum of distress:.................................. 151

Anxiety and Excitement 153

There are several external causes of anxiety: 154

Distress, overwhelm, anxiety, trauma, and beyond... 156

Precaution to passing on the 'Empowered Butterfly Method': 159

Let's build trauma-informed communities 161

Building Trust and what does trust truly mean? 163

This is an introduction to the ethos to consider when building relationships to make a difference in the world of others: 163

People tend to approach trust differently. 164

The four domains we can assess to re-build trust, by Charles Feltman 167

Be trained and create a hope-filled world 168

The Empowered Butterfly Method draws from a well of Techniques Including but not limited to: 171

Epilogue: 173

Caution Disclaimer: 179

Want to support our upcoming publications, get involved: 181

Orientation

Welcome to the Empowered Community
We hope this message finds you well, as filling your own cup is essential before embarking on helping others.

We would like to bring attention to an important issue that affects many individuals and families: suicide. It is a difficult topic to talk about, and many of us have been touched by a loved one struggling with mental health. Some of us had the terrible news of another not finding any other straws but ending their lives.

We believe that we can reverse the trend by raising awareness about this epidemic and diverting the thought process early on by using the *Empowered Butterfly Method*.

By fostering communications within our communities, awareness, and connections are able to can grow exponentially.

Successful communities evolved from communication.

This keystone seems to be being rapidly eroded in modern society, with increased use of screens and decreased eye contact.

Our goal is to make suicide a very unappealing option by lessening the pain inside. With warm, safe spaces created, the pain is allowed to be expressed and shared. Knowing you are not alone in your pain can give you a feeling of security.

We also recognize that reaching out to someone who may be struggling with thoughts of suicide can feel as if we are imposing. That's why we want to equip all communities with tools and resources to meet people in distress more gracefully, confidently, and impactfully.

Just as with 'The Heimlich Maneuver,' knowing how to respond in an emergency can save someone's life.

Similarly, if we have the knowledge and skills to approach someone who may be struggling with suicidal thoughts, we can save their life.

We understand that stepping up and reaching out to someone in need is uncomfortable, but this discomfort is nothing compared to the guilt of knowing that we could have made a difference if only we had acted. That guilt can last the rest of your life.

Let us work together to build the community so that we are confident and equipped to respond early rather than waiting only to react to those in desperate need. By responding early, we can make a difference in many people's lives worldwide.

Let's build our interactive web strong and wide, supporting each other along the way.

Thank you for your attention, dedication, and willingness to spread the message of this important cause.

Please share your wins and challenges with us so we may restore the vital keystone of caring communication in our communities.

Imagine that...

Warmly, Your *Empowered Butterfly Method* Team

What is The Empowered Butterfly Method?

- Quickly transforms feelings of worthlessness to hope.

- Combines multiple methodologies with body movements in rapid succession.

- Proven intervention to reduce stress.

- Developed to deal with suicide ideation and has been found worthwhile in many stressful situations

- Beneficial for everyone who finds themselves in a supporting role.

- For professionals (physicians, psychiatrists, nurses, and social workers), the Butterfly Method was approved for 0.5 hours of continuing education at the International Summit on Psychiatry and mental health, a Star-Icon conference.

Why We Wrote This Book

Did you really want to die?" "No one commits suicide because they want to die." "Then why do they do it?" "Because they want to stop the pain. - **Tiffanie DeBartolo**

B oth of us could so easily have become 'just' another statistic. One in five Americans choose to cut their lives short. That is 2 - 3 times the number of alcoholics. Each of the deaths by suicide is a tragedy, but so many more reach the verge of despair as we did in that critical moment. It is impossible to estimate how many people around us have had suicidal attempts or ideas. This is a pandemic that needs to be reversed. By reaching people before they have suicidal attempts and supporting them, we are letting them know they aren't alone.

We knew something had to change, and together we can promote a powerful method that has the potential to reach far with your help.

We are striving to provide a training program in the *Empowered Butterfly Method* so you, too, can become an ambassador for hope. We also develop easy and largely free tools for communities to get involved. Schools will be able to apply for a training package as part of their mental health weeks to have a lasting effect and to get older kids to teach the youngest, with daily reminders at strategic places throughout the building to create a system that works, from initial tool to use in the toilets, fostering conversations building the confidence needed to reach out to have the right support at hand.

Keep an eye out, share your story, and help us grow at:
www.empoweredbutterflymethod.com

www.facebook.com/EmpoweredButterflyMethod

Patricia Kaine MD

My family is riddled with people who have died by suicide. This includes two paternal aunts, two maternal cousins, and my sister. Thus, I deeply know the pain of a family member who has 'been left behind.'

With these experiences, people may be surprised that I also have a long personal history of suicidal ideation. It coincides with some of the suicides I mentioned. I also had a history of 'needing to be right,' so I never mentioned it. I had been raised with the belief that suicide was 'wrong.' However, I lived with suicide being an option for everything. On a regular basis, when needed to make a choice, one of the choices would always be committing suicide.

When my desire 'to end it all' became so intense that I knew I was not safe to be alone with 'me,' I chose hospitalization to protect me from myself.

'The Original Butterfly Method' was developed during a time of four hospitalizations over a 12-year period. Utilizing 'The Original Butterfly Method,' I have been able to transform from suicidal thoughts to hope and positivity in the time it takes to go to the bathroom. Many days I have had to repeat this several times. Fortunately, nature has designed us to get rid of physical waste from our bodies a few times every day. Utilizing this time to eliminate 'mental waste' only makes sense.

I've taught 'The Original Butterfly Method' to patients and others for over three decades. When I shared or taught 'The Butterfly Method,' I was silent about my story. As a physician, I was able to 'get away with this' because society elevated me to a level of authority, so people were willing to listen to me.

Even years after developing and using The Butterfly Method, suicide seemed available as an option in many situations. It became easier to dismiss suicide as a poor (or inappropriate) choice as my neural pathway strengthened. In November 2019, I was convinced that I was short-changing many people by not sharing my personal story and limiting teaching 'The Butterfly Method' to one person at a time in private.

I enrolled in a course to facilitate public speaking, which I finished in February 2020. My plan was to share 'The Original Butterfly Method' during orientation week for colleges and universities. I would expand the message when school was in session by speaking at high schools.

Covid necessitated a pivot. I was 'forced' to learn ZOOM! As time passed, I became convinced of the need for a book. It was on the ZOOM platform that I met my fabulous co-author, Simone Moir. Our personalities aligned, and you just know when you know working together is right.

Simone Moir

I met Patricia at a great time of growth; as fate had it, we ended up in a virtual room together. We both share the gift of the gap and receive messages from what we refer to as the divine. It was clear that we had a future together, and it became clear that this book would bring us together.

I had a near-death experience in my teens, which changed my life forever, as behind the veil, all questions most people chase answers to, have been answered for me. I spent my life enjoying my bonus round and following the clear guidance I am blessed to receive.

Being of service and allowing my gifts to benefit those who align with me is not just a passion; it's my vocation and calling.

Throughout my life, I have been in a place close to death and suicide, as if it magically gravitated to me.

I am not afraid to die or talk about it.

I have experience being present during the sacred dying process, and I'm also part of a thresholding community that supports individuals at the end of life. We've been able to continue our work during the pandemic by providing well-received, remote spiritual support through prayer and song.

Additionally, I often find myself as a source of support for individuals who feel that ending their life may be their only option, turning this around with them using the tools shared here and compassion.

Working with the Public Foster Service, especially young adults, gave me the opportunity to provide often harshly abandoned children with the tools in this book, equipping them to embark on their independent lives.

We, as a society, seldom speak about suicide. It gives us shivers, and it is largely taboo, as it makes us uncomfortable. Individuals that came close to it often do have a wish or even a need to speak about it and are surprisingly comfortable doing so.

Having someone who is willing to explore alternative options with you while still acknowledging that ending life may be one of the choices on the table can feel liberating and empowering. As Dr. Patricia Kaine mentioned in her introduction, considering the option of ending one's life is often a prominent thought, and there is no need to pretend that it isn't.

Once, I had come close. I understand how it can happen to anyone from any walk of life, background, and culture.

Disconnecting from Self frequently leads to disconnecting from society and support. Keeping up a false facade is all too common and seems easier than reaching out. Substances and other ways of escapism corrupt our thinking further, and soon enough, ENDING IT ALL seems the best way out of the pain building up inside. For me, it felt like I was taken to the train tracks to end my life, as by an invisible force, it was certainly not a conscious decision or choice I made to end my life.

I am honored and privileged to now work with Dr. Patricia Kaine, a truly heartfelt connection. A woman rich in experience both professionally and personally to bring her life's work to you.

I have been successfully working with the tools in this book since the tender age of 12, deeply intuitively understanding their purpose and power.

My love for simplicity, organic and playful application met fertile ground, and teaching so a 5-year-old can understand has been my passion ever since, by using simple metaphors, graphics, maybe edgy language, and simplifying to the essence.

The 'Empowered' was gifted through me to make The Original nine organic steps even easier to remember without fail.

My vision is that each copy sold, a seed of deeper understanding is planted, so we can catch the first wobbles in and around us with graceful ease.

May **The Butterfly Method** and the following books in this series become a household name, taught in schools and communities, so you too can have a "how to..." guide to meeting hopeless or suicidal thoughts in a supportive manner.

E.M.P.O.W.E.R.E.D

Why You Should Read The 'Empowered Butterfly Method'

A must-read for anyone, as YOU TOO can be the one that saves a life or that returns someone lost - back to hope.

Just as it is vitally important to know the ABC method of First Aid for a person's physical health, it is vitally important to know The *Empowered Butterfly Method* for mental health.

All we sometimes need is to stop, be aware, and be willing to act.

When we experience despair, the tunnel of perception is narrowed.

It can become so much that ending our life seems like the best choice. This is the definition of suicidal ideation.

What we need is a trusted and caring person to help us stop and gain new tools so that, in time, we have a strong, deeply embedded alternative that is pro-life.

Some philosophers and psychologists seem to think that the opposite of depression is actually play. Play is defined as any behavior that involves pleasure or seeking new people and experiences.

It is vital that the community, businesses, schools, church, or youth clubs are skilled in facilitating communication about emotional distress and ways to alleviate it.

We need to move this from a Taboo-Topic to one that is safe to share and has a space in our society.

9-steps
Done is better than
perfect

Stats and Figures

Suicide is a permanent solution to a temporary problem. - **Phil Donahue**

We do not need to refer to statistical reports to show you how common and important mental health problems are. Most of us know someone, maybe a close friend or a relative, who dealt with such issues. However, when we are experiencing suicidal thoughts, it is easy to believe that we are the only one who feels this way. The numbers clearly show that we are not alone.

According to the CDC, more than 46 thousand people took their own life in 2021 in the United States. It is hard to imagine what this number means, but we can think of it as 126 deaths per day. Compared to that, road accidents caused around 117 deaths (NHTSA).

However, these numbers only tell us how many people died by suicide, and it is impossible to know exactly how many attempted or considered taking their own lives. A large-scale study that looked at young university students in the US found that 8% of them reported experiencing suicidal thoughts and behaviors (Paul et al., 2015). Interestingly, another study from England reported much higher numbers. According to them, 1 in 5 people have dealt with suicidal thoughts at one point in their life (NHS Digital). It is hard to say why these results are so different, but it might be because the British study included more people from low-income backgrounds, a factor often associated with a higher rate of mental health problems.

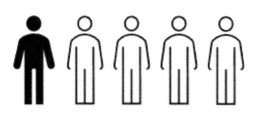

In 2019, a fifth of hospitalized children (aged 3 to 17) were admitted because of mental health reasons. 64% was due to attempted suicide or self-injury (**Arakelyan et al., 2023**).

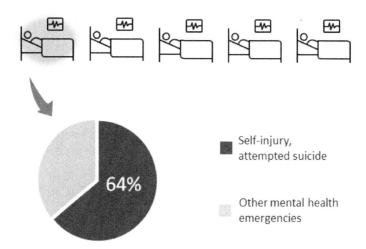

During the pandemic, we all experienced how quickly our circumstances can change. Although suicide rates did not increase, uncertainty and loss had a bad effect on our mental health (Pirkis et al., 2021). At the beginning of the lockdown, depression, anxiety, and suicidal ideation became more common due to the financial and health concerns the pandemic brought. Even if we do not take into consideration one's health and social status, isolation can double the chance of developing depression (Henssler, 2021). It had an even more significant impact on people who were already vulnerable, such as unpaid carers, victims of domestic violence, or disabled people.

This shows us that we need to have tools that effectively help our mental health since the rapidly changing world we live in can test our resilience any day.

During our lifetime, anxiety and stress-related disorders are the most common forms of mental illness and among the largest health burdens in society (Kessler et al., 2005). Yet current treatment approaches fall short: rates of quality 'care' using a combination of cognitive behavioral therapy (CBT) and pharmacological treatments are low (Stein et al., 2005), and symptom recurrence remains high with as many as 60% of patients symptomatic after one year (Olatunji et al., 2007; Westen et al., 2004). Thus, there is a pressing public health and scientific need for the development and refinement of interventions for anxiety that are both low-barrier, and that potentially target novel mechanisms underlying the emergence and maintenance of anxiety disorders.

We need less treatment of a disorder and more community to grow mental fitness, agility, and health.

How To Get The Most Out Of The Method:

K.I.S.S.
Keep It Super Simple

Learn it - Practise it - Share it

The most important part of the method is to catch yourself and STOP. This is one of the reasons this method needs to be practiced before you need it.

Make it part of your day. Take your natural rhythms as an invitation to practice a minimum of 3 times per day.

In this way, we can lock in the new habit so it turns on automatically in a time of need.

As we know, when a person is triggered, the brain reduces to its fight or flight reaction, adrenaline rushes, and you no longer have access to your higher reasoning faculties.

This is why it is important to have this developed as a habit.

The Butterfly Method is designed to lock together in an organic, logical sequence to transition from negativity to hope.

It can be a quick rescue or used as a supportive mental health program that can be learned step-by-step by someone caring for a vulnerable person as well as by the person themself.

Being the personal example often is more effective than 'telling someone what their choices should be.
If a person is overwhelmed, they can often still follow logical, simple instructions. The more the *Empowered Butterfly Method* is practiced, the more ingrained it becomes as an automatic response.

If this is not effective, seek immediate professional help. Most countries and many communities have helplines you can call.

Find out and save it in your phone right now, well before it's needed.

If your community does not have a dedicated mental health line, Call your country's emergency number.

The *Empowered Butterfly Method* is like throwing a lifebuoy to a person in a river. If the person is able to grab hold and follow the instructions, The *Empowered Butterfly Method* is an option. If not, it is essential to call emergency services
As with everything else, being aware and alert is crucial-catching and responding to the first signs is most important.

To name a few examples of distress, which always are an invitation to start a conversation and check in.

- disturbed sleeping patterns

- skipping meals or bingeing

- persistent mood swings

- choosing seclusion

- avoiding talking about feelings

- withdrawing from activities

or ANY OTHER change in the person's normal behavior
If you notice ANY of these changes in the person and you sense something may be going on, trust your gut instinct. This is always a good reason to connect and create a safe listening space.

Many times all a person needs to know is that someone cares enough to take an interest in them.

Schools and communities need to work better collaboratively since a child is not raised exclusively by one individual but by their entire community.

In our modern life, working together towards a unified goal is not common and mental health suffers greatly. With increased interactions through mobile devices, the ability to recognize and vocalize the more subtle emotional changes is being lost. Therefore, adults need to become aware of the increased need to make an extra effort for connections and act on it.

It should be the role of the more mature or stable person to initiate and build connections.

Rebuilding families, interest groups, and communities is vital!

The combination of these tools has been shown to be a powerful method and can be used as a self-help tool to help manage many situations. With more practice, the more entrenched the neural pathways become in time. Even more severe cases of distress can be effectively controlled than could be when first starting this practice.

These tools need to be practiced outside of times when negativity is the trigger in order to embed them as a default. Thus, it is suggested they are utilized on every visit to the bathroom.

Download the easy-to-follow card to keep near you at all times. **www.empoweredbutterflymethod.com**

scan for free
talk-through
audio

1. **EXIT** - Say, "I need to go to the bathroom."

2. **MOVE** - Deep Abdominal Breathing

3. **PIVOT** - Redirect your mind with "I am relaxed" Mantra

4. **ON & OFF** - Tighten and relax all muscles sequentially.

5. **WAY OUT** - Picture all your stress leaving into the toilet.

6. **ENVISION** - Picture yourself in your happy place

7. **RELEASE** - Flush the negativity away.

8. **END THE OLD** - Wash the rest of stress away

9. **DO THE NEW** - Walk with a smile and a plan. Otherwise, call someone

The Stages of the *Empowered Butterfly Method* in 3 Sections

There is a story behind why I refer to the transformation of suicide ideation to hope as The *Empowered Butterfly Method*.

1 Caterpillar

When I was challenged with suicidal thoughts, I felt like a caterpillar. I considered myself as being not liked or appreciated (even by me). I believed I was a pest and worthless. People often try to get rid of caterpillars to stop them from destroying plants.

The only value many people see in caterpillars is stomping on them and turning them into fertilizer. In the same way, I thought the world would be better without me. Taking my life would achieve this.

My value was in ceasing to live.

2. Cocoon

However, everything changes when the caterpillar enters the cocoon. It is alone. It is transforming. The negativity associated with its previous state also metamorphoses into something desired.

Using this analogy, the caterpillar conceals itself in a cocoon as it goes through a transformation.

Self-preservation and **transformation** tend to be private experiences.
I found by escaping into the bathroom; I could transform my thought process by utilizing the techniques I had learned during my hospitalizations. The bathroom was a safe 'cocoon' where I could quickly do what worked in rapid succession without drawing attention to myself.

3. Butterfly

A beautiful butterfly emerges from the cocoon.

I emerge from the bathroom with the beauty of hope by focusing on my happy place.

There is a variety of butterflies, uniquely beautiful. Each of us is also different. Therefore, when emerging from the bathroom, expect to be in 'your' better place, which cannot be compared to anyone else. If it is calming to you, it is right.

Summary QUICK OVERVIEW

EXIT Strategy = Stop (WILL)

Action: STOP and say: "I need to go to the bathroom."

Well done - This step is the first and maybe the hardest because it forces you to speak up and express a need. Fortunately, society is accustomed to saying 'yes.' You are well on your way to the safe haven you have created.

OVE   Move body and breath (LIFE FORCE) Action: Walk away from despair:

Place one hand on your chest and one hand on your abdomen.

If the hand on your abdomen is moving, you're taking deep breaths. If the hand on your chest is moving, breathe deeper. Let the breath follow the bottom hand.

ivot   Pivot your mind (ENERGY)

Action: Say in your head this mantra:

"I am" on the inhale - "relaxed" on the exhale.

When you get to the bathroom, assume the seated position on the toilet.

    On/Off button - Progressive relaxation (PHYSICAL)

Action: Gain control over your body

Tighten and relax your muscles one group at a time from feet to head.

40

Way out – Visualization (MENTAL)
Action: Away it goes
Picture all stressful thoughts, sensations, and emotions leaving your mind, traveling down your spine, and going into the commode.

nvision

Envision your happy place (VISUAL)
Action: Picture yourself in your happy:
Creating a safe place, you can return to any time using all your senses to feel like you are there.

Release (Auditory)
Action: Flush the negative down the toilet - Let go.
Enjoy the sound of change; you no longer are holding all the burden inside.

nd old

End of old (Tactile)
Action: washing your hands:
Cleanse yourself of distress while energizing your system, entering a clean, positive place.

Do the new with a smile (Muscle Memory)
Action: Walking towards hope:
The positive choice you decide to do right away.
Plan to go to your happy place or call someone.

41

The Butterfly Method

Deep Dive
Section 1 The Caterpillar

Chapter 1

EXIT Strategy = Stop (WILL)
Quick Action: STOP and say: "I need to go to the bathroom."

Well done - This step is the first and maybe the hardest because it forces you to speak up and express a need. Fortunately, society is accustomed to saying 'yes.' You are well on your way to the safe haven you have created.

E - Stands for Exit

Let's take it deeper:

STOP and excuse yourself to the facilities.

When triggered by confrontation or stressful situations and you notice your thoughts slipping down the 'suicidal ideation' slide or going towards depression, excuse yourself to the bathroom.

'Stop Practice' is a used and proven tool in Cognitive Behavioral Therapy.

It is used as the first step onto a new and safe path to confront your triggers which is why 'The Butterfly Method' begins with it.

You will see little resistance from your environment when you ask for the restroom. This is your escape route into a safe space where you can close the door behind you and gather thoughts, emotions, and pictures to turn things around.

What is it?

The "stop" method in psychology is used to interrupt or disrupt negative thoughts or behaviors. It is a cognitive-behavioral strategy that can be used to counteract automatic or habitual responses that may be causing distress or impairment. The goal of the stop method is to interrupt the thought or behavior and replace it with a more positive or adaptive one. The technique involves using a specific word or phrase, such as "stop" or "no," to interrupt the negative thought or behavior and then redirecting the focus to something positive or constructive.

It's a fun, quick and easy-to-learn technique. Use it first as a tool to say 'STOP' and notice. As with anything new, consistent practice is required.

Sometimes the situation needs to be stopped as it's triggering or hostile.

In our society, saying 'Stop' often is unacceptable, yet saying "I need to go to the bathroom" will rarely meet resistance and will accomplish the needed action of exiting the situation.

Randomly practice it throughout the day, so the neural pathway that is responsible for applying the brakes can become stronger. Even a few days of practice will make stopping a strong possibility when triggered. For it to become your default response, it takes more practice.

How to do it?

Stop what is happening by excusing yourself from the bathroom.

Explore this practice to gain a deeper understanding:

STOP ACRONYM STANDS FOR:
S: Stop.
Whatever you're doing, just pause momentarily.

T: Take a breath.

Reconnect with your breath. The breath is an anchor to the present moment.

O: Observe.

Notice what is happening.

What is distressing or causing you to be uncomfortable?

What is happening inside you and outside of you?

Where has your mind gone?

What do you feel?

What are you doing or not doing?

P: Proceed. If necessary, exit the situation.

Use the information gained at this check-in to adjust your course.

Choose to continue what you were doing (or not doing) if it's positive:

If it's negative, continue with part 2 of this step-by-step path to a calmer, more grounded you.

Why does it work?

Thought-Stopping Techniques

You have a 60-second window to make a new decision. This process interrupts the 'automatic pilot' and allows you to become present enough to make alternative choices to gradually change the path of your life.

Why is it included?

To change any old pathway of habit, you need to stop and realize what it is you are doing first in order to be able to make a new, better choice toward your empowered life.

The benefits of the "stop" method in psychology include:

1. Interrupting negative thoughts or behaviors: The "stop" method can be used to interrupt negative thoughts or behaviors that may be causing distress or impairment.

2. Reducing distress: By interrupting negative thoughts or behaviors, the "stop" method can help individuals reduce feelings of anxiety, depression, or other forms of distress.

3. Enhancing focus: Using the "stop" method can help individuals redirect their focus to something positive or constructive, which can improve overall focus and concentration.

4. Improving mood: By interrupting negative thoughts or behaviors and redirecting the focus to something positive, the "stop" method can improve overall mood and well-being.

5. Enhancing self-control: The "stop" method can be used to increase self-control by interrupting negative thoughts or behaviors and redirecting the focus to something positive or constructive.

6. Enhancing cognitive flexibility: The "stop" method can help to enhance cognitive flexibility by interrupting negative thoughts or behaviors and redirecting the focus to something positive, promoting the ability to switch between different tasks or thoughts.

It is important to note that the "stop" method is not a stand-alone treatment and should be used in conjunction with the other included strategies for best results.

This is why it is the first step in The Butterfly Method. When going at high speed in an unfavorable direction, it's wise to stop first before course-correcting so you don't spin out of control.

Example

Patricia's Story Police Whistle

When we hear a police whistle, everyone stops and pays closer attention to the surroundings before proceeding. It's the quickest way to avoid harm.

Thought-Stopping Techniques

In most cultures, no one will stop you.

You need to stop yourself.

The most important part of the method is to catch yourself and STOP. This is one of the reasons this method needs to be practiced before you actually need it.

Make it part of your day. To develop this habit, set your alarm to 3 random times in your day. This way, when it rings, 'STOP' what you're doing and assess whether you should proceed or pivot. Take this opportunity to strengthen this new neural pathway and EXIT your usual flow of thought.

When you are triggered into fight, flight, or freeze, your brain reduces to a more primitive brain. Adrenaline rushes, and you have no access to your higher faculties any longer.

When is the best time to stop a car from rolling down the hill?
Is it at the top or the bottom of the hill?

Well, that is why taking the edge off by calming yourself with the *Empowered Butterfly Method* can be seen as stopping the car before it had a chance to pick up too much momentum.

Affirming this new toilet habit keeps your breaks in optimal condition.

If you are well hydrated (something we strongly recommend), there is no need to remember to practice or set an alarm. Your body will assist you with that gladly. You will STOP what you're doing and answer 'nature's call.' It's built-in. In the beginning, you might only remember the rest of the steps in The Butterfly Method when you actually sit on the commode... but that is totally fine.

This is where you break the cycle.

Celebrate and mentally pat yourself on the back or do a little happy dance as the words come out of your mouth.

The first 60 seconds are the most important. You are more than on your way to finding calm, even though it might not look like it just yet.

The more often you do it, the more you build trust that this process will work.

Questions that might come up in Chapter 1:

What if I can't find the right moment to exit?

What if my confidence leaves me?

What if I can't manage to get a word out?

Answer to all three questions:

That is why practicing the exit step in advance of needing it is beneficial. It is natural for people to resist doing something new. This is why these questions are arising. The answer is to tell yourself: "I can EXIT this ONE time."

Expect your brain to go to what it knows best – RESISTANCE! Any move in a new direction is a threat. If you understand this, you will understand why it has to be rehearsed. The brain learns to accept this strategy as a known option and will no longer perceive it as a threat.

Research links and Further reading

1. The Relaxation & Stress Reduction Workbook by Martha Davis, Ph.D., Elizabeth Robbins Eshelman, M.S.W, Mathew McKay, Ph.D., published by New Harbinger Publication. 7th Edition 2019

2. "Cognitive Behavioural Therapy for Adults with Attention Deficit Hyperactivity Disorder (ADHD)" by J. Russell Ramsay and Anthony L. Rostain, published in the Journal of Clinical Psychology in 2008.

3. "Feeling Good: The New Mood Therapy" by David D. Burns, M.D. (Harper, 1999)

4. "Mind Over Mood: Change How You Feel by Changing the Way You Think" by Dennis Greenberger and Christine A. Padesky (The Guilford Press, 2015)

5. "The Cognitive Behavioral Workbook for Anxiety: A Step-by-Step Program" by William J. Knaus and Jon Carlson (New Harbinger Publications, 2014)

6. "Retrain Your Brain: Cognitive Behavioral Therapy in 7 Weeks: A Workbook for Managing Depression and Anxiety" by Seth J. Gillihan, Ph.D. (Althea Press, 2019)

Chapter 2

M ove body and breath (LIFE FORCE)
Quick Action: Walk away from despair:
Place one hand on your chest and one hand on your abdomen.

If the hand on your abdomen is moving, you're taking deep breaths. If the hand on your chest is moving, breathe deeper. Let the breath follow the bottom hand.

The M in empowered stands for Move

(or it could also stand for multitasking).

Let's dive deeper

While walking to the bathroom, place one hand on your chest and one hand on your abdomen. Let the breath flow to the hand on your abdomen, which will then rise and fall with the deep tummy breathing. If the hand on your chest is moving and following your breath, breathe deeper. On the inhale, think, 'I am.' On the exhale, think 'Relaxed.'

What it is

Moving out of the distressing environment is vital.

The immediate environment influences what happens in the mind.

My thoughts at home tend to be very different than when I'm in a forest, office, car, or store.

Granted, distressing thoughts can occur in any of these places. However, moving to a different area causes the mind to readjust, which is helpful in a quick transformation.

While moving to the bathroom, one hand is on your chest and the other on your abdomen. You'll be deep breathing while concentrating on a relaxing mantra.

Controlling your breath has been fashionable since the beginning of time. We have learned that breathing fast can warm us up, breathing slowly can cool us down, and that, in return, affects our energy levels, emotions, and mental state.

The people who can control their breath can control their minds.

In modern times, we've disconnected from this instinctual knowledge and have not been taught how effective our breath really is when battling against our inner world.

If any of these exercises help quickly when mastered, breath work is the one.

Breathing in and out slowly helps regulate our nervous system. The deeper the breath goes into the belly, the better.

You can use it right away with the instructions below and gain benefits right away. Patience and persistence will pay off.

How to do it:

As you walk to the bathroom, put one hand on your belly and one on your chest.

Invite your breath down into your belly as deeply as you can.

Breathing in and out slowly.

Explore this practice to gain a deeper understanding:

Let's start by seeing what we've got first.

It's easiest to learn this deep breathing technique by either lying on the floor with your knees bent or sitting upright on a chair for now rather than while you're walking.

We have an inhale and an exhale - that's clear. The third part of our breath is often missed, and that is what gets us spinning in the hamster wheel, unable to stop.

One at a time:

Our Inhale:

Bring one hand to your abdomen and one to your chest. Even if you find this strange, I would highly recommend it, as it brings you into your body.

'I feel me' keeps you grounded in knowing that you are right here right now and not going anywhere for now. Touching the 'heart' and 'belly' is unifying, helps you become present, and brings your thoughts into the here and now.

Remember to do this in a safe space.

A toilet is another easy option when practicing deep breathing for the first few times (developing the neural pathway).

Breathe through your nose, allowing it time to get warmed by the nostrils, humidified, and partly filtered; this is like smelling your favorite scent.

Notice:

Which hand do you notice moving when you breathe?

Is it the hand on top (on the chest) or bottom (on the abdomen)?

What helps you breathe deeper?

Invite your breath down deep to allow your bottom hand to be gently moved up and down. This may seem tricky as it just shows that your default is putting a lot of pressure on your nervous system by keeping you in fight or flight, which might be a new response for you.

However, this can quickly get you from tense to calm.

This changes with a little bit of practice. Your breath goes where your attention goes. Imagine how it would feel if your tummy could balloon and just invite the breath to follow that invitation (no force needed).

On the Exhale:

Allow your tummy to sink back to your spine, and notice how much air comes out.

In fight and flight, people tend to inhale longer than they exhale... it's surprising that we don't explode.

This also shows how much we hold onto stale air.

CAUTION:

When emptying your lungs, you might feel slight nausea or dizziness as your body is not used to having room for fresh air. This will pass.

This is why we recommend starting out sitting on a chair or lying on the floor.
When the lungs feel 'empty,' try artificially coughing as much as you can (without drawing more air in). Out - out - out with the stale air, pause, then enjoy the fresh air flooding back in.

Our Pause:

Ahh.. here we go .. who knew?

Yes, there is a pause that should precede each exhalation. I could write an entire book just on this, but just will give you a little story later on.

Breathing ... Modern society has it all wrong! Why did no one tell us? Our body should come with a user manual!

Diaphragmatic breathing is also referred to as horizontal breathing when you breathe correctly, as your diaphragm moves and assists in the filling and emptying of the lungs.

The lower ribcage expands out, which gives it the name 'horizontal breathing.'

Shallow breathing is referred to as vertical breathing. It becomes the default breathing when in fight-and-flight mode.

Your inhalation is effortful, moving your shoulders and upper chest only. When you look at yourself in the mirror, your shoulders and chest rise (vertically up) when you inhale and then drop when you exhale (vertically down).

What is a horizontal breath?
You inhale into good posture as it fills the bottom of the lungs first and completely, your back, as well as the bottom of your chest (horizontally). You will notice your belly extending out.

The exhalation allows the diaphragm to empty out the lungs effectively, but as the diaphragm is a muscle that might not have had much of a workout ... give it some time to play and find its purpose.

And by breathing from the tummy and pushing out the exhalation, we assist the diaphragm in reclaiming its natural job.

We have many mis-recruited muscles attached to our breathing, all doing a job they were never built for.

We tend to use the intercostal muscles more than the diaphragm when we breathe, as we often slouch and breath shallow.

When we breathe into our abdomen, we recruit the correct breathing muscles.

Often that's the reason why we are low on energy and feel close to death when waking up in the morning... we merely survived the night due to shallow- vertical breathing habits. Often falling into mouth breathing, we inhibit the quality of our breathing habits.

What happens:

An additional benefit to diaphragmatic breathing is that it lowers your blood pressure.

Here's what happens when you do this easy breathing exercise:

Let's look at the anatomy of stress for a moment:

The autonomic nervous system (which is an involuntary reflex) responds in two different settings. There is the "fight, flight or freeze" mode and the "rest and digest" mode. The "fight, flight, or freeze" mode helps you focus and prepare an appropriate response when you feel threatened, and the "rest and digest" mode helps you relax and digest thoughts, food, and emotions.

The vagus nerve is associated with the "rest and digest" mode and helps you relax and restore. It also helps lower your defenses and sets the stage for social interaction and lasting change.

First, you begin to calm your sympathetic nervous system (known as your fight, flight, or freeze response). This lowers the feelings and hormones of stress.

The vagus nerve is like a wandering highway that starts at the nape of your neck, runs down the sides of your neck, and wanders through all the vital organs in your body. It's called the "wanderer" because it connects everything from your brain to your vital circulatory, digestive and reproductive organs.

The vagus nerve touches all of the bodily systems except for the adrenal and thyroid glands. Overstimulation of the adrenal gland can put a strain on the body. The vagus nerve helps boost the immune system, lowers stress, and regulates inflammation. It creates a feedback loop back to our brain, which is also referred to as the gut instinct.

With deep abdominal breathing, the diaphragm moves up and down, which facilitates blood flow toward the heart and stimulates the vagus nerve.

Example

Simone's Experience

Having been a Yoga Therapist for over 25 years, I found that people with chronic stress might still be struggling with belly breathing after this introduction.

Here are some additional tips to play with:

Imagine you're smelling your air instead of taking a breath; close your eyes and envision smelling a flower or lemon.

Two things might happen

Your mouth starts watering (a good sign as that shows your parasympathetic nervous system, which is also known as your 'rest and digest' setting, has taken control - that's good news, by the way, more on that later in the book.)

Sometimes adding a little weight, such as a pillow or a hot water bottle on the belly, helps identify the correct muscles for deep breathing when you are lying on the floor.

The main active breathing muscle called the diaphragm, is a sheet-like muscle separating the lungs and the abdomen horizontally.

Reclaim your sanity breath.

If your intercostal muscles, the slim layer of muscles between your ribs, are tight from holding tension for years or aftershocks, that can also contribute to this being more challenging.

You might want to try some rounds of pretend coughing or shaking your body wildly to help loosen them up.

Why it works

Breath is life!

We can only go a few minutes without it, and we expire. Poor breathing is usually overlooked when searching for possible reasons for feeling low, tense, or even hopeless.

Poor breathing diminishes the flow of oxygen and carbon dioxide to and from your body, putting your body in an alarming situation. This contributes to anxiety, panic, depression, muscle tension, headaches, fatigue, and more.

Good breathing habits will benefit your physical, spiritual, and mental well-being.

If you struggle with emptying the lungs completely and you are prepared with the first suggestion of breathing out -out -out, explore blowing out of your mouth with pursed lips downward.

This is like blowing into a bottle to make a sound, maybe something you played with as a child. You may try this and explore different water levels to play a tune.

This has been proven to lower your cortisol levels (stress hormones) within minutes and is fun.

Why it is included

Breath is the most powerful tool we have for regulating the body, mind, emotions, and our connection to something greater than us. A tool worth investigating deeper!

Belly breathing, also known as diaphragmatic breathing or horizontal breathing, can be an effective technique to soothe panic. The benefits of belly breathing for panic include:

1. Reduces stress and anxiety: Deep breathing helps reduce the stress response in the body by slowing down your heart rate, lowering blood pressure, and reducing the level of stress hormones in your bloodstream.

2. Improves physical health: Deep breathing can help improve lung function and increase the amount of oxygen in the blood. It can also help strengthen the diaphragm and other respiratory muscles, which can improve overall respiratory health.

3. Enhances mental clarity and focus: By calming the mind and reducing stress and anxiety, deep breathing can help enhance mental clarity and focus.

4. Promotes relaxation: Deep breathing activates the parasympathetic nervous system, which is responsible for promoting relaxation and calming the body.

5. Boosts immune system: Deep breathing can help boost the immune system by reducing stress and anxiety, which are known to weaken the immune system.

Questions that might come up in Chapter 2:

My breath does not get past my upper chest. What should I do?

Blow all your breath out. Cough more out. Then take in a deep breath, visualizing your lower chest expanding. As with all new activities, it takes practice to have the muscles become accustomed to moving.

Research Links and Further Reading

1. Book: The Relaxation & Stress Reduction Workbook by Martha Davis, Ph.D., Elizabeth Robbins Eshelman M.S.W, Mathew McKay, Ph.D., published by New Harbinger Publication. 7th Edition 2019

2. "The Healing Power of the Breath: Simple Techniques to Reduce Stress and Anxiety, Enhance Concentration, and Balance Your Emotions" by Richard Brown and Patricia Gerbarg. Shambhala Publications, 2012.

3. "Breath: The New Science of a Lost Art" by James Nestor. Riverhead Books, 2020.

4. "The Breathing Book: Good Health and Vitality Through Essential Breath Work" by Donna Farhi. Holt Paperbacks, 1996.

5. Busch V, Magerl W, Kern U, Haas J, Hajak G, Eichhammer P. The effect of deep and slow breathing on pain perception, autonomic activity, and mood processing--an experimental study. Pain Med. 2012 Jun https://pubmed.ncbi.nlm.nih.gov/21939499

6. Ma, X., Yue, Z. Q., Gong, Z. Q., Zhang, H., Duan, N. Y., Shi, Y. T., Wei, G. X. (2017). The Effect of Diaphragmatic Breathing on Attention and Stress in Healthy Adults. https://www.ncbi.nlm.nih.gov/pmc/articles/PMC5 455070

These papers can be found in most research databases, such as Pubmed, ScienceDirect, and SpringerLink.

Chapter 3

This life. This night. Your story. Your pain. Your hope.
It matters. All of it matters. — **Jamie Tworkowski**

Pivot your mind (ENERGY)

Quick Action: Say in your head this mantra:

"I am" on the inhale - "relaxed" on the exhale.

When you get to the bathroom, assume the seated position.

'P' in empowered stands for pivot

Let's dive deeper

All change involves pivoting.

Say in your head this mantra

"I am" on the inhale

"relaxed" on the exhale

What it is

If a person realizes that he is traveling in the wrong direction when driving, he must pivot to be able to reach his desired destination. The sooner he realizes the error and pivots, the less damage and loss of time. With the STOP demand, we have taken the momentum out. Now it's time to reinforce the course correction.

When a person has suicidal thoughts, it is necessary to pivot by changing the thought pattern. One way to do this quickly is with a mantra.

In 'The Butterfly Method, ' we use the mantra 'I am relaxed'... very slowly.

On the inhale, think 'I am,' and on the exhale, think 'relaxed.' We begin this while walking to the bathroom and continue it throughout the entire time of practicing *'The Butterfly Method.'*

The use of simple mantras combined with slowed breathing can be an effective technique for managing feelings of despair. Mantras are short, positive phrases or words that are repeated to oneself as a form of self-talk.

How to do it?

When you become aware of your breath

Think of the words 'I am' when you inhale

and the word 'relaxed' when you the exhale

Why it works

A few breaths in through the nose and out lowers your cortisol levels significantly.

This stress hormone is responsible for your vision to narrow and blood to move out of your frontal lobe (the prefrontal cortex - where we make educated decisions) to the reptilian part of the ancient brain where fight and flight was a well-needed response to danger.

Nowadays, dangers and fears tend to be more prolonged, turning chronic. This is due to a variety of factors, including the fast pace of society, instantaneous global news, continuous repetition of calamities, etc.

These seldom warrant the strong reptilian response of fight or flight yet trigger them more than ever, causing fatigue, overwhelm, and confusion.

Settling your breath and then calming your thoughts by directing them is a great way to calm your neuro pathways and prepare for the next steps.

Why is it included?

The combination of mantras with slowed breathing can provide a number of benefits, such as:

1. Reducing negative thoughts: Mantras can serve as a form of cognitive restructuring, helping to replace negative thoughts with positive affirmations. This can be especially helpful when in a state of despair, as negative thoughts and self-talk can be exacerbated.

2. Calming the mind: Using the mantra while slowing down the breath is a form of diaphragmatic breathing that can help to calm the mind and reduce feelings of anxiety and stress.

3. Enhancing focus: Repeating mantras while focusing on the breath can help to increase focus and concentration, helping individuals to stay present in the moment.

4. Increasing self-awareness: Using mantras and slowed breathing together can increase self-awareness, helping individuals to change negative

thoughts and patterns of behavior that may be contributing to feelings of despair.

5. Improving mood: The combination of mantras and slowed breathing can help to improve overall mood and well-being, reducing feelings of despair.

Example - Story

Patricia's Experience

(As a child, you learn through repetition)

Mom says to brush your teeth before you go to bed.

This becomes automatic to the point that it is impossible to fall asleep in bed if you haven't brushed your teeth. Taming your mind is like putting the reins on. When your limited capacity to think clearly is taken over by a mantra, no other thought can budge in.

It buys time and creates space to get you to your safe space.

The breath and the mind are closely interlinked. Most people find it easier to tame the breath than the mind. Straw breathing is a well-researched technique that communicates directly with your amygdala and sends a sense of "all is good" into your brain.

Questions that might come up in Chapter 3:

My mind keeps racing. What can I do?

This is expected, which is why it is so important to practice breathing with the mantra 'I am' on the inhale and 'relaxed' on the exhale.

This can be done multiple times of the day, i.e., when grocery shopping or waiting for transport, climbing steps...

With practice and the development of the neural-pathway, In time, the racing will slow down.

What if I am relaxed and cannot be further from the truth, and I can't seem to say this and mean it?

You don't need to believe it for it to work.

However, you can choose another word or mantra that has calm energy attached to it for you:

I am calmer

I am walking

I am breathing

Research Links And Further Reading

1. The Relaxation & Stress Reduction Workbook by Martha Davis, Ph.D., Elizabeth Robbins Eshelman, M.S.W, Mathew McKay, Ph.D., published by New Harbinger Publication all 6 Editions 2019

2. "The Art of Happiness" by the Dalai Lama and Howard C. Cutler, published by Riverhead Books in 1998. This book includes a section on the use of mantras in meditation and mindfulness practices.

3. "Mantras Made Easy" by Sherianna Boyle, published by Adams Media in 2018. This book provides guidance on how to use mantras for stress reduction and mindfulness, including the use of simple mantras to calm the mind.

4. "The Science of Mantras: How Sacred Sounds Heal Body, Mind, and Spirit" by Rajendar Menen, published by New World Library in 2019. This book provides an overview of the science behind mantra meditation and includes guidance on the use of mantras for stress reduction and mental well-being.

5. "Mantra Meditation: An Alternative Treatment for Anxiety and Depression" by E. Ospina et al., published in the Journal of Evidence-Based Complementary & Alternative Medicine in 2012.

The Butterfly Method

Section 2 - The Cocoon

Chapter 4

O n/Off button - Progressive relaxation (PHYSICAL)

Quick Action: Gain control over your body

Tighten and relax your muscles one group at a time from feet to head. ON/OFF button - Progressive relaxation (PHYSICAL)

79

The 'O' in empowered stands for on and off

Let's dive deeper

In *'The Butterfly Method, '* it correlates with progressive relaxation.

Assume the sitting position on the toilet as if you are planning to use it.

Tighten and relax your muscles in sequence (starting with the feet and progressing to the head). First, become aware of your feet on the ground, squeeze to tense (on) with the inhale and relax (off) them with your exhale.
Remember to continue your mantra

Inhale - I am

Exhale – Relaxed

Progress up your legs, buttock, back, and tummy while taking the deep, slow abdominal breaths

Continue to your chest and shoulders squeeze, then relax,

make fists and tighten your arms, then relax,

allow your face to scrunch up, then relax.

Let your head droop and allow yourself to feel like a ragdoll in the process, if that feels right, allowing your back to relax while still holding onto the breathing practice and affirmational mantra from the previous steps.

With practice, progressive relaxation becomes so familiar that you can become as limp as a ragdoll quickly.

What is it?

The body responds to anxiety-provoking events with muscle tension. This, in turn, messes with our breathing and thinking. This has an effect on all our bodily functions and imprisons us in fight-flight or freeze responses of our alarmed sympathetic nervous system. Tightened muscles trap negativity, which is why it is vital to relax them.
No Imagination or willpower is required to learn this technique.

Progressive relaxation is a technique that involves tensing and then relaxing various muscle groups in the body. It is a form of relaxation therapy that aims to reduce tension and stress by promoting physical and mental relaxation.

The technique typically begins with tensing a muscle group, such as the muscles in the feet, and then holding the tension for a few seconds before relaxing the muscles and focusing on the sensation of relaxation.

This process is repeated for each muscle group, starting with the feet and moving up the body to the head.

Progressive relaxation can also be done while sitting or lying down whenever needed.

It is more effective when accompanied by deep breathing, as this enhances relaxation.

Progressive relaxation has been found to be effective in reducing muscle tension, anxiety, insomnia, and other stress-related symptoms.

With practice, this might feel something like a slow release throughout your body, like air being slowly released from a balloon. You might feel like you're collapsing slowly into a limp state like a deflated balloon.

This can also be used separately from The Butterfly Method (as a stand-alone activity) to ground a wired-up state of body and mind.

How to do it?

You will see why it takes practice, as there is quite a bit to it.

We are deliberately using multiple techniques simultaneously to develop new neural pathways for this to become automatic, swift, and readily available.

In Summary:

You start at the bottom

Tighten the muscles in your feet while inhaling, holding your breath for a moment, then while exhaling, relax the muscles in the feet... continue focusing on different muscle groups while going up your body, staying symmetrical until all your muscles are relaxed. Allow all of the tension (muscle tightness) to leave you.

This can be practiced in many places, such as lying in bed, sitting on the edge of your bed, as well as other places to build this muscle memory. Important side note: Progressive Relaxation (outside of The Butterfly Method) is taught as a stand-alone activity, and the sphincter muscles are skipped. Thus, as long as you remember you are NOT on the toilet, you will be fine, and accidents should be kept at bay.

Explore this practice on its own to gain a deeper understanding.

Can you use progressive relaxation as a way to go to sleep at night?
The answer is Yes. That's why we show you the lying down in bed option.

In 'The Butterfly Method, ' we deliberately progressively relax from feet to head. This way, we bring energy into your head to stimulate our neuro-channels.

The head to toes variation is designed to be more sedating to promote sleep. It is also more grounding.

Scrunch up and adjust the intensity of the squeeze to your ability and liking.

By visualizing your body part by part, bit by bit, breath by breath, drop into a more relaxed stage. You can literally see or envision sleep and calm coming over you.

Start:

Feel your scalp and face muscles being pulled up - inhale, squeeze tighter, hold your breath squeeze more, and exhale slowly. You may play with adding a sound if you wish, such as a deep sigh-like sound - haaaa, whatever feels right in the moment.

Many people are drawn to yawn at this point. If you feel a yawn coming on, embrace it, milk it, as it is one of the signs that you successfully shifted into your parasympathetic nervous system.

Relaxing all those muscles, letting your head droop.
Notice the contrast - pause and release urgency.
(With time, you notice your eyes, jaw, and lips all wanting to have a squeeze so you can go into more detail and take more breaths as you wish)

Continue the progressive relaxation with your shoulders and arms, including fists, biceps, and forearms - inhale, squeeze tighter, hold your breath squeeze more, and exhale slowly as above, relaxing all those muscles.

Notice the shoulders dropping with the pull of gravity.

Again be aware of the contrast - release any urgency.

Fill your lungs to nearly bursting. Have your chest and upper back expand like the Incredible Hulk, feeling your belly expand, hold your breath, and exhale as above, relaxing all those muscles.

Sinking into your bed when lying or when sitting, feel your muscles collapsing from the upper back.

Again become aware of any change - pause, release any urgency.

Place your hands on your abdomen, inhale, hold your breath, and exhale slowly, squeezing out all the stale air in whichever way feels best at the moment.

Softening the belly.

Again become aware of any change - pause and release any urgency.

Continue down the body by tightening the buttocks, then the thighs, lower legs, and feet - inhale, squeeze tighter, hold your breath, and exhale, relaxing all those muscles to allow them to feel jelly-like.

Once more, become aware of any changes - pause and release any urgency.

Welcome the comfortable warmth and heaviness of deep relaxation traveling throughout your whole body.

OPTIONAL:

Lastly, collect all remaining tension into one last big squeeze - inhale, squeeze tighter, hold your breath, and exhale slowly, relaxing every muscle. Enjoy the total limpness.

Invite the looseness and relaxation from your head and shoulders throughout your body to your feet.

Stay relaxed, calm, and rested for a few more breaths.

From this place, you may rest in bed and fall into a relaxing sleep, or you may gently return to the awareness of the day feeling refreshed. Take your time coming back.

You might feel dizzy from the increased oxygenation of your blood, so avoid standing abruptly. This will pass with a few breaths.

Hold onto the feeling of peace, calm, and relaxation as if you could program it into your subconscious, bottling it for the next time you might need a little sip of this.
We invite you to drink some water to hydrate and wake up more completely. Dehydration is an unnecessary stressor to the body.

Why it works?

Deep muscle relaxation reduces physical tension and is incompatible with anxiety. When practiced, this puts you in the driver's seat of your body, being able to choose to tense or relax your body at will.

It has been taught in the military as a way to find rest periodically, even while at the front line. It has been proven especially helpful with fighter jet pilots as they need 100% focus and precision. They need to sleep when back at base, even if adrenaline is pumping through their bodies after having been a prime flying target.

Why is it included?

It works.

The benefits of progressive relaxation include:

1. Reducing muscle tension: Progressive relaxation helps to release muscle tension that can be caused by stress and anxiety.

2. Reducing anxiety: Progressive relaxation can be effective in reducing anxiety symptoms by promoting relaxation and reducing muscle tension.

3. Improving sleep: Progressive relaxation can be helpful in improving sleep quality by reducing muscle tension and promoting relaxation.

4. Improving overall well-being: Progressive relaxation can improve overall well-being by reducing stress and tension in the body, which can lead to improved mood and energy levels.

5. Enhancing self-awareness: Progressive relaxation can help individuals become more aware of their bodily sensations, which can aid in the identification of muscle tension and stress triggers.

6. Improving cardiovascular health: Progressive relaxation can help to lower blood pressure and heart rate, which can improve cardiovascular health.

7. Improving immune function: Progressive relaxation can help to improve immune function by reducing stress and tension in the body.

Example - Story

Patricia's Experience

I learned progressive relaxation during my first hospitalization for suicidal ideation. Every day, we would go to the all-purpose room with mats for a period of progressive relaxation. It lasted for 20 - 30 minutes. Our instructor was very laid-back and gentle. It was very calming to me. By tightening my muscles and relaxing them, I felt more in control of many things, including my suicidal thoughts.

Being able to lay on individual mats with several other people, all also having positive results, was very enlightening to me. Some of the patients actually fell asleep during it. That shows how relaxing progressive relaxation was for them.

Over the decades, I have kept up the practice of progressive relaxation. However, since that time, I've also modified it for better utilization in '*The Butterfly Method*.'

This enabled similar results while allowing it to be done more quickly.

It has been very helpful with the suicidal ideation part of my life to have this as a tool.

Knowing that there are modalities, in addition to Western medicine, that work for various different issues broadened my horizons.

When a person is distressed, being able to relax causes a very good outcome.

Questions that might come up in Chapter 4:

Why is it so important to practice this outside of The Butterfly Method?

To make this an automatic response in your subconscious. My body has become so accustomed to the importance of relaxed muscles aiding in removing the mind of distressing thoughts that with the command 'ragdoll,' my body becomes limp.
It's a bit like the STOP command. The more it is ingrained in your cellular memory, the more effective it is when you need it. It literally becomes a switch button.

Why does it seem so hard?

This is the most challenging step in The Butterfly Method. It involves the entire body sequentially. It has the most steps and needs a longer practice time to develop a neural pathway before it becomes automatic. The more you do it, the more automatic it becomes.

Research links and Further reading

- The Relaxation & Stress Reduction Workbook by Martha Davis, Ph.D., Elizabeth Robbins Eshelman, M.S.W, Mathew McKay, Ph.D., published by New Harbinger Publication all 6 Editions 2019

- "Relaxation techniques for stress management: Stress inoculation training for the workplace" by Daniel P. Newman, Sarah M. Harrison, and Kristin D. Dashner, published in the Journal of Organizational Behavior Management in 2015.

- "Progressive Relaxation" by Edmund Jacobson, M.D., published by University of Chicago Press. This book, originally published in 1938, is considered a classic and pioneering work in the field of relaxation techniques.

- "The Relaxation Response" by Herbert Benson, M.D., published by HarperCollins Publishers. This book, originally published in 1975, introduces the concept of the "relaxation response" and provides step-by-step instructions for practicing progressive relaxation.

Chapter 5

Way out – Visualization (MENTAL)
Action: Away it goes
Picture all stressful thoughts, sensations, and emotions leaving your mind, traveling down your spine, and going into the commode.

W in empowerment stands for Way Out

What is it?

Visualization is calling pictures up in your mind's eye.

We've practiced visualization from the time we were infants. We saw something we wanted, visualized our hand reaching for it, and were rewarded when we grasped it. As we grew, we visualized walking by, watching those older than us, and imitating their example. Children create numerous visualizations in their play, seeing themselves achieving what their heroes succeed in doing.

We all do it, even by recalling any past event. There is a direct line between these pictures and your body. For example, thinking of your favorite food does make your mouth water.

It is a powerful tool, when used with awareness, that can save your life literally.

Unless you can SEE yourself doing something, it's hard to make it happen.

The vision of it precedes most actions.

Make sure to take a moment to give yourself credit for embracing a new skill.

We shall use several visualization techniques and will explore them one by one

The "let go and release" visualization technique is a form of guided visualization that involves mentally letting go of negative thoughts, emotions, and physical sensations that may be causing stress and tension.

This technique can be helpful for individuals who are experiencing feelings of despair, anxiety, or stress.

Visualization is a sensation-led release.

Visualization is a technique that involves using the imagination (inner eyes used in daydreaming) to create mental images, sensations, and feelings in order to achieve a desired outcome.

In the context of mental health, visualization is often used as a tool to help individuals let go of stress, anxiety, and other negative sensations and emotions.

How to do it?

See the negative stressors that are currently affecting you in a distressing way. Get a clear mental picture of them. Visualize them, leaving your brain and racing down your spine and being eliminated by depositing them in the commode just like you deposit physical waste products. Continue picturing all this mental negativity leaving until there is none left.

Why does it work?

We are offering a unique combination of an actual physical letting go with visualization, which increases its effectiveness manyfold.

Why is it included?

The benefits of the "let go and release" visualization technique include:

1. Reducing stress and anxiety: By letting go of negative thoughts, emotions, and physical sensations, we are making space for the positive, like relaxation and peace, which also helps to reduce stress and anxiety.

2. Enhancing self-awareness: By releasing stubborn negative thoughts, emotions, and physical sensations, one can become more aware of what triggers these feelings. This can then help identify and address the underlying issues.

3. Improving sleep: By promoting relaxation and reducing stress and anxiety, visualization can help to improve sleep quality.

4. Improving focus and concentration: Individuals can improve focus and concentration by focusing on visualization. This helps them stay present in the moment, integrating body, mind, and spirit.

5. Improving cardiovascular health: visualization of letting go can help to lower blood pressure and heart rate, which improves cardiovascular health.

6. Improving immune function: visualization can help to improve immune function by reducing stress and tension in the body.

7. Improving bladder function: This is recognized in TCM (Traditional Chinese Medicine) as the flow of Chi (life force energy) is affected by the emotion of fear or anxiety.

Example - story

Patricia's Experience

The mind is amazing. What it visualizes in the imagination seems as real as what is actually happening.
When I go to the movie theatre, I am sitting in a seat. However, my mind draws me into the movie on the screen.

I laugh, cry, or experience other emotions with the characters in the movie. My mind has me behaving as if I'm IN the movie, although I KNOW I'm sitting in a seat in the theatre eating popcorn. This also frequently happens when I'm reading an interesting book or watching 'Lassie' or another sitcom on the television. (I know that last example dates me!)

Thus, at this step, after being totally relaxed, I visualize the mental 'crap' leaving my brain, traveling down my spinal cord, and emptying into the commode. For me, seeing this leaving my brain by the most direct route, I feel it traveling down my spinal cord and hear it 'plopping' into the commode. Yes, sometimes it smells very stinky. Often, I have to visualize this more than once. That's logical and normal. Think about it. Emptying the bowels of physical 'crap' often takes more than one push, and sometimes it stinks.

Questions that might come up in Chapter 5:

Why are you so graphic?

Our brains operate with pictures. The more detailed, the easier it is for the brain to create a clear picture of the desired outcome. The more graphic, the quicker the response. Also, the more precise, the easier it is for the brain to follow the appropriate neuronal pathway.
I wanted to leave the suicidal thoughts behind as completely as possible.

Can I do this away from the commode?

After the neural pathway is developed, yes.

Research and Further Reading

1. Book: The Relaxation & Stress Reduction Workbook by Martha Davis, Ph.D., Elizabeth Robbins Eshelman, M.S.W, Mathew McKay, Ph.D., published by New Harbinger Publication all 6 Editions 2019

2. "Full Catastrophe Living: Using the Wisdom of Your Body and Mind to Face Stress, Pain, and Illness" by Jon Kabat-Zinn, published by Delta (1990).

3. "The Body Bears the Burden: Trauma, Dissociation, and Disease" by Robert Scaer, published by Routledge (2007).

4. "The Relaxation Response" by Herbert Benson, published by William Morrow Paperbacks (2000).

5. "Guided Imagery for Self-Healing" by Martin L. Rossman, published by H J Kramer (2000).

6. "The Mindfulness Solution: Everyday Practices for Everyday Problems" by Ronald D. Siegel, published by The Guilford Press (2010).

Chapter 6

nvision

E nvision your happy place (VISUAL – Imagery)

Action: Picture yourself in your happy place:

Creating a safe place, you can return to any time using all your senses to feel like you are there.

The 2nd E in empowered stands for Envision

Let's go deeper

Using imagination to envision and create (revisit) your anchor or happy place.

Recruiting our S.M.I.L.E. = Special Magic In Living Everyday reinforces imagery.

What is it?

Filling the void - after emptying the negative, we need to fill in with something positive, or the negative will return to its familiar place.

Making a movie of your happy place will fill the space.

Stepping into it with as many senses as possible will reinforce it to stay longer.

The step after pivoting is 180 degrees opposite from the thoughts when entering the bathroom.

Going to my happy place in my imagination looks like this:

It is on the side of the mountain in late spring. There is a babbling brook passing through fields of flowers.

I'm smelling the fragrances, listening to the birds, and feeling the breeze on my cheek.

By dipping my hands into the clean, cool stream, I can bring a taste of the freshwater to my lips. That sip touches every cell of me with the essence of contentment.

The peace and joy permeate my soul.

What's your happy place?

Experience the details in your mind, and feel free to explore various places. Choose the one that feels safest, where you can return to it over and over. This will reinforce the new positive neural pathways.

How to do it?

As you are already physically relaxed (thanks to the previous steps), the mantra has tamed your mind, and you also find yourself breathing more deeply. You're well on your way to enjoying your happy place.

When setting out to create your special place, be curious and playful. No one else needs to love it except you.

It's your special place. Smiling while doing this intensifies the experience. It's common to become aware of increased moisture in your mouth. This is a sign of your body that it feels safe.

Consider these features:

This place might be indoors or outside.
Connecting our body, mind, and spirit to natural surroundings grounds us and is beneficial to a long-term solution.

Make a secure private entrance, so no one else can intrude.

Make it peaceful, comfortable, and safe.

Fill your place with sensuous details pleasing to the eyes, with a delightful scent, a relaxing sound in the background for your ears, and tantalizing textures.

Create a 3D depth by establishing a foreground, midground, and backdrop, yet enveloping you.
Allow space around you.

Do not change it every time you go. Keep it predictable and recognizable so your nervous system knows exactly what to expect, where you will settle, and how it all feels there.

Why does it work?

1. Reducing anxiety and stress: By picturing a safe space in your mind, you can create a sense of calm and relaxation that can help to reduce anxiety and stress levels.

2. Increasing feelings of safety and security: Imagining a safe space can help you feel more secure and safe in your mind, which can lead to greater feelings of comfort and peace.

3. Enhancing mindfulness and self-awareness: Imagining a safe space requires you to focus on the present moment, which can enhance mindfulness and self-awareness.

4. Encouraging positive thinking: When you picture a safe space in your mind, you can also focus on positive thoughts and emotions, which shifts your mood and perspective.

5. Improving coping skills: By creating a safe space in your mind, you can develop new coping skills that you can use in real-life situations when you feel anxious or stressed.

6. Improving mood: The imagery of a peaceful and calming place can help to improve mood and overall well-being by promoting relaxation and reducing negative thoughts and emotions.

7. Switch on Ease: By dropping into your Parasympathetic Nervous System, you connect to calming emotions and hormones.

Why does it work?

The power of imagery far exceeds the power of will alone. It is hard to relax yourself into relaxation. Have you ever had someone tell you, "Relax, it won't hurt..." just to find yourself tenser after that comment?

This will become a place of ultimate comfort, and as we are creatures of comfort, it will draw us there with ease.

Also known as guided imagery or mental imagery, this technique involves using the imagination to create mental images, sensations, and feelings in order to achieve a desired state.

In the context of mental health, imagery is often used as a tool to help individuals cope with or temporarily escape stress, anxiety, and other negative emotions. The technique involves mentally creating a peaceful or positive scene and focusing on the details of that scene, such as colors, sounds, taste, touch, and smells, in order to create a detailed sense of relaxation and well-being.

Why is it included?

The power of imagining positive things automatically engages the parasympathetic nervous system, which is calming and restful. When closing your eyes and going to bed, all your body knows are the images in your head. If your thoughts create a frightful picture, the sympathetic nervous system, your fight, flight, or freeze response, kicks in. This is why it's important to choose the opposite 'right setting,' which is the calming, happy place.

Here in this scenario:

It is so important to practice this while you are in a physically safe environment. Doing it in an undisturbed safe space is the key. Because you can lock the door, the bathroom is a safe space to practice this.

Example

Patricia's Story

I always use Imagery when I need a dental procedure.
I am physically in the dental chair with my mouth open.
However, actually, in my mind, I'm on the side of a mountain.

I see the wispy clouds in the sky contrasted with the meadow flowers near me.

I smell the fragrance of the flowers.

I hear the birds singing and the brook babbling.

I feel the breeze on my cheeks.

As I sit by the brook descending the mountain, I scoop up some of the clear water in my hands.

I bring this cool refreshment to my lips and sip in the freshwater enjoying the taste.

My dentist has learned I'm oblivious to her while she is working as I choose to focus on my happy place.

Questions that might come up in Chapter 6:

I can't imagine a happy place. I'm not sure what this is like. Can you guide me further?

First, you must be in a safe place. This is a place where you can have a few uninterrupted minutes, which is why I've chosen the bathroom. Some people can use their bedroom, a car, or a secluded place outdoors. What is important is that it's a place you can relax.

Some people are challenged to find a happy place from their actual past experiences. If this is the case for you, think, have you ever wished to be someplace from a movie or book? People wish for what they want because it brings happiness. Go there in vivid detail.

Why is it important to include the different senses?
The more senses that are involved, the more neural pathways are activated. This creates a longer-lasting response.

References and Further Reading

1. Book: The Relaxation & Stress Reduction Workbook by Martha Davis, Ph.D., Elizabeth Robbins Eshelman, M.S.W, Mathew McKay, Ph.D., published by New Harbinger Publication all 6 Editions 2019

2. "Guided Imagery for Self-Healing" by Martin Rossman, published by HJ Kramer in 2000.

3. "Cognitive Behavioural Therapy: A Teach Yourself Guide" by Christine Wilding and Stephen Palmer, published by Hodder Education - 2013

4. "The Body Keeps the Score" by Bessel van der Kolk, MD, published by Penguin Books - 2014

5. "Mind Over Mood" by Dennis Greenberger and Christine A. Padesky, published by The Guilford Press - 2015

Chapter 7

The pain passes, but the beauty remains. – **Pierre August Renoir**

Release (Auditory)
Quick Action: Flush the negative down the toilet - Let go.

Enjoy the sound of change. You no longer are holding all the burden inside.

R- stands for release, to get rid of completely

Let's go deeper

Proceed with your usual rituals for completing the business.
Follow this with flushing the toilet.

What is it?

When flushing the commode, the waste is released into the sewer.

Our subconscious automatically associates the sound of flushing to complete the riddance of the waste material in the commode.
Thus the sound of the flushing confirms through the sense of hearing the complete removal of the mental crap.

This completes removing the negativity, which has been replaced with happy thoughts.

Being asked to 'Let things go' can be a paralyzing process as we want to hold onto what is familiar. Flushing is a simple process of replacing a distressing familiar with a familiar of getting rid of the unwanted. It is using a neural pathway that has already been formed. It's a button we are familiar with.

The action, sound, and intention form a new possibility for allowing all or most of the previous tension to go somewhere else, with no need to drag it outside the bathroom.

This takes the weight off your shoulders. Knowing that when you flushed it, you no longer carry it. This is powerful.
This can lift your spirit and translate into a lighter step and better posture.

How to do it?

Flush the toilet and know it's done.

The sound reinforces the command to flush it all away.

Again, by involving additional senses, neuronal pathways are strengthened.

It's not just wishful thinking.

Why does it work?

Using an audible cue, such as a particular sound, to manage stress or signify moving on can lead to several changes in the brain that promote relaxation and emotional regulation.

The activation of the parasympathetic nervous system can reduce heart rate, blood pressure, and respiration rate, while the regulation of the amygdala can reduce feelings of anxiety and fear.

The activation of the prefrontal cortex can lead to greater cognitive control over emotional responses, and the release of endorphins can enhance feelings of well-being and relaxation.

Additionally, the use of an audible cue to include truly ALL senses promotes neural plasticity, leading to the development of new neural pathways that support positive behaviors and emotional regulation.

Overall, the use of all sensual cues is a powerful tool for managing stress, promoting relaxation, and facilitating emotional regulation.

Fear responses in an infant happen only from sudden changes
1. Loud sound

2. Being dropped

3. Bright light impulses

Our sound sense is directly linked to our survival instinct from pre-birth. Infants in the womb respond to sound.

Why is it included?

When used after this process of letting go, it signifies moving on or leaving behind the past. Associating the flushing sound with this process can have additional benefits, including

1. Symbolic meaning: The sound associated with moving on or leaving behind the past can have

symbolic meaning, representing closure, completion, and a new beginning.

2. Emotional release: The sound can act as a signal to release emotions associated with the past, providing a cathartic experience that can help to let go of all the mental baggage.

3. Encouraging positive change: The sound associated with moving on can inspire a sense of optimism and motivation, encouraging positive change and growth.

4. Boosting self-esteem: The use of an audible cue to signal to move on can provide a sense of closure and accomplishment and boost self-esteem, reinforcing a person's ability to overcome challenges.

5. Neural plasticity: The use of an audible cue to signify moving on or leaving behind the past can help to promote neural plasticity, the brain's ability to adapt and change. This can lead to new neural pathways that support positive behaviors and emotional regulation.

6. Promoting self-care: The sound can act as a reminder to prioritize self-care and prioritize one's well-being moving forward.

Example - Story

Patricia's Story

"Every time the bell rings, an angel gets its wings" from 'It's a Wonderful Life' or Pavlov's dog experiments (see below) are obvious examples of how automatic response to sound is. Have you ever been in a crowded room with multiple conversations going on? From somewhere across the room, you hear your name, and immediately you're attentive to that particular conversation.

By associating an action, you can see and feel a specific noise with imagery (you might be lucky and get the smell in there as well - do not even try to add taste, please). We establish a neuro anchor. Doing this several times a day builds a solid neural pathway at fiberoptic speed.

Even though these exercises are all easy, taking the time to develop the neural pathways consistently is another kettle of fish altogether.

We talk ourselves out of taking new actions.
The good thing about this toilet routine is that you flush every time, and you will naturally go to the next step of washing your hands.

These habits have already formed since childhood and do not trigger a foreign response to our nervous system. They're safe and tested!

We merely add a little thought, an organic concept to ride along with it.

Flushing is the sound of you nailing this.

Pavlov's Dog

In the early 20th century, a Russian scientist named Ivan Pavlov conducted a famous experiment involving dogs. Pavlov noticed that the dogs in his laboratory would begin to salivate as soon as they saw the lab assistants who fed them, even before any food was presented. He hypothesized that the dogs had learned to associate the lab assistants with the food.

To test this hypothesis, Pavlov rang a bell each time the dogs were given food. After several repetitions of this process, the dogs began to salivate at the sound of the bell, even if no food was present. This demonstrated that the dogs had learned to associate the sound of the bell with the arrival of food and that this association had become automatic.

This experiment became known as the "Pavlovian" or "classical conditioning" experiment, and it has been influential in the fields of psychology, behaviorism, and neuroscience. Pavlov's work demonstrated that many forms of behavior could be learned and modified through association and that even seemingly involuntary responses like salivation can be conditioned.

Questions that might come up in Chapter 7:

What if I have a waterless toilet?

Good point.

You can use the sound of the lid closing, or you have the option to clap your hands instead of flushing or to make a noise or move associated with the end of this step. You're allowed to be creative. What works for you?

References And Reading List

1. "Atomic Habits: An Easy & Proven Way to Build Good Habits & Break Bad Ones" by James Clear. Published by Avery in 2018, this book explores the science behind habit formation and provides practical strategies for making lasting changes using sensory cues.

2. "The Power of Habit: Why We Do What We Do in Life and Business" by Charles Duhigg. Published by Random House in 2012, this book examines the neuroscience behind habit formation and provides insights into how changing habits can have a profound impact on our lives.

3. "The One Thing: The Surprisingly Simple Truth Behind Extraordinary Results" by Gary Keller and Jay Papasan. Published by Bard Press in 2013, this book emphasizes the importance of focusing on

one key habit or behavior change at a time and provides practical strategies for achieving success.

4. "Tiny Habits: The Small Changes That Change Everything" by BJ Fogg. Published by Houghton Mifflin Harcourt in 2019, this book explores the concept of "tiny habits" and how making small, incremental changes can lead to significant improvements in our lives. It includes strategies for using sensory cues and other techniques to create lasting habit change.

5. 101 Miracles of Natural Healing by Chan, Luke was published by Square One Publishers in 2007.

Chapter 8

You can either be crushed by a horrific event and lose your sanity, your <u>family</u>, and your life. Or, you can take this pain that was thrust upon you to propel you into greatness. You can make it through this. I know it's hard. — **Marie White**

End of old (Tactile)

Action: washing your hands:

Cleanse yourself of duress while energizing your system, entering a clean, positive place.

The final E in empowered stands for END ALL

Let's go deeper

Wash your hands slowly and mindfully. Give attention to each finger and to your palms.

What is it?

We complete the step of 'The Butterfly Method' of using the commode by washing our hands in a slow and mindful way.
This brings the 'Sense Of Touch' into the transformational experience. The more senses are involved, the more the experience is cemented into the subconscious.

Again, the subconscious is already programmed into knowing hand washing completes leaving the waste behind.

Simply lathering up your hands and washing them while commanding:
This is it! I have chosen to leave the past behind.

Cleansing yourself, allowing the last morsels of tension to leave by soaping up and rinsing it away.

Again it relies on your intention and visualizing skills we have practiced throughout this method.

How to do it?

"Washing your hands" slowly and mindfully is used as an action to establish a clear and defined end to our powerful sequence and to signal the transition to moving on with the day.

With this action, we are starting anew and totally cleansed.

This action can serve as a physical reminder that 'The Butterfly Method' is complete.

Now it's time to return to daily activities with a positive perspective.
The act of washing hands can also serve as a grounding technique, helping to bring one back to the present moment and to wash away any lingering thoughts or emotions from this session.

By washing hands, the person is symbolically washing away any negative leftover thoughts and emotions that they let go of during the process and is now ready to move forward.

This action acts as an anchor, helping to embed the positive effects of *'The Butterfly Method'* in the person's mind and makes it easier to recall and utilize the positive feelings in their daily lives.

Here is one more opportunity to soothe and strengthen your Parasympathetic nervous system, this time with cold water.

If you have the option of using cold water, you get the additional benefit of stimulating your Vagus nerve.

In the Vagal theory, the colder the water, the more the Vagus nerve is stimulated. In this study, temperatures of 50°F were considered cold.

Research found that an increase in blood flow to your body and brain warms the tissue, improves nerve connectivity, and turns on your relaxation response (parasympathetic nervous system

Additional research confirmed that when the body adjusts to cold temperatures, your fight-or-flight response (sympathetic nervous system) declines, and your rest-and-digest response (parasympathetic system) increases.
No need to go wild swimming. Just cooling your face and the back and sides of your neck are already affecting the vagus nerve. Simply splashing cold water on your face and neck, even just gently stroking your face, has shown mild benefits.

Why does it work?

It's a strong sensation, stimulating and embedding your command

Visually (look at your hands)

Auditory (sound of squishing & washing)

Olfactory (smell of soap)

sensation (of touching yourself, feeling the soap and water)

DO NOT LICK THE SOAP, please!

Rather notice your mouth feeling sweet and moist with the relaxation response.

By paying attention to washing each finger, we incorporate energy medicine.

Energetic stimulation is widely researched and accepted as powerful.

It's instinctual. Infants suck their thumb to soothe themselves, even pre-birth.
If you rub each finger one by one, you also stimulate your body's energy flow and many pressure points that help you circulate CHI (life force energy) through your system.

Stuck CHI is a side effect when we panic.

It's time to get it flowing again.

Your hands have energy lines that affect every body function. These are referred to in TCM (Traditional Chinese Medicine) as meridians.

Jin Shin Jytsu (Japanese healing art) has conducted research on simply holding or rubbing each finger, the palms, and the wrists, which has been shown to support mental health.

Why it is included

This is another powerful psycho-sensory tool that involves touch.

It's used as an additional anchor and embodiment tool to seal the process.

Do you remember this all started with you saying STOP?

1. Helping to bring the individual back to the present moment: Washing your hands can serve as a grounding technique to release any lingering thoughts or emotions from the session.

2. Creating a clear end to the session: The act of washing your hands can serve as a physical signal that the session has now ended and it's time to return to daily activities as an empowered person.

3. Anchoring positive effects of 'The Butterfly Method': The individual is now ready to move forward. This acts as a cellular anchoring effect in the person's mind and body. This makes it easier for them to recall and utilize the positive feelings in their daily lives.

4. Reducing anxiety and stress: Grounding techniques such as washing your hands help bring the person back to the present moment, which helps to promote a sense of relaxation and well-being.

5. Improving focus and concentration: Grounding techniques can help to improve focus and

concentration by bringing the individual back to the present moment and helping them to stay present in the moment.

6.   Stimulating the body's Chi - each finger holds the key to shift energy and, therefore, emotions (Jin Shin Jutsu - Japanese Art of healing)

7.   Positive cold water effects, alongside the tactile stimulation of rubbing the hands together, can activate the parasympathetic nervous system (vagus nerve), triggering the body's relaxation response and reducing feelings of tension and stress.

Example - Story

Simone's Experience

Making *'The Butterfly Method'* the ultimate habit-stacking sequence

When it comes to building new habits, you can use the 'connection of behavior' to your advantage. One of the best ways to build a new habit is to identify a current daily habit and then stack your new behavior on top. This is called habit stacking.

I came across people that are ashamed to say that even tooth brushing is not certain and that habit stacking will not work.

This is the ingenious part of 'The Butterfly Method' Nature is calling you guaranteed without fail to visit the facilities at least 3x a day.

Washing your hands of responsibility: by washing your hands, the remaining stress is cleansed away

Look into the mirror and be proud of yourself.

Questions that might come up in Chapter 8

I just can't visualize what should I do?

I am still so tense. What should I do?

This is when professional help is needed. Call a help hotline or go to an emergency room. If you are already established with a mental health person or agency, follow the advice you have been given.

EMERGENCY NUMBERS: Check to see if your country has a mental health helpline and save the right one to your phone now and encourage others to do so as well.

References and Further Reading

1. "The Power of Touch: The Basis for Survival, Health, Intimacy, and Emotional Well-Being" by Phyllis K. Davis, published by Healing Arts Press in 1999.

2. "The Magic of Touch: Revolutionary Ways to Use Your Most Powerful Sense" by William Benko, published by Warner Books in 1997.

3. "The Touch Remedy: Hands-On Solutions to De-Stress Your Life" by Michelle Ebbin, published by HarperCollins in 2016.

4. "The art of hands-on-healing," Mary Burmeister, published by Himalaya Institute in 1980

The Butterfly Method

Section 3 - The Butterfly

Chapter 9

D o the new with a smile (Muscle Memory)

Quick Action: Walking towards hope:

The positive choice you decide to do right away.

Plan to go to your happy place or call someone.

D in empowered stands for
Do the new

Let's go deeper

Change is only solidified when the NEW is practiced.

Before leaving the bathroom, have a plan to go to your happy place, share your thoughts about your happy place with someone, or simply write or draw in a journal about your happy place.

Allow your walk to express your positive shift by walking taller and more purposeful with your shoulders relaxed.

Focus on your hope as a smile on your face emanates from your transformation.

Witness how YOU have just transitioned from distress to hope.

It Is easy to miss a slow spiral down,

Dr. Patricia Kaine has found a 'Mood Chart useful as a powerful tool for keeping track of her distress/good days.

We designed a simpler version, especially for your easy tracking.

Available to download here.
www.empoweredbutterflymethod.com
'My mood checker' - A 1-sheet monthly overview

If you are still having challenges, seek professional help.

What is it?

A deliberate and empowered physical (somatic) action piece of changing your course upon leaving the bathroom.

This way, you overwrite your default and build strong new ways of looking at the situation from a taller, stronger, and more resourced perspective.

You are meeting the situation more grounded and physically taller, as well as energetically recharged.

By showing up differently and making a choice pro-change, you empower yourself to break old chains and choose freedom.

How it works:

If the positive change becomes the path of least resistance, by nature, our lazy mind will go there by default.

The former negative path may be well-trodden, but the positive path is calling you, and therefore even though muscle building takes practice, an exhilarating adventure is awaiting you.

Repeated practice develops the emotional agility needed to ascend these banks of resistance, becoming truly empowered.

'The Butterfly Method' is a rope to help you become confident in navigating life with more grace.

Enjoying these new heights, which one might be experiencing for the first time, presents a positive perspective on life and is a beacon for others.

Why does it work?

Reclaiming your willpower and asserting yourself awakes your life force.

Even changing your posture has an impact on how you feel and how other people perceive you. Not dropping your head brings more oxygen to your brain. Standing upright makes you take in more air which invites the wind of change on a physical level.

Making a decision, no matter how little, and following through is an amazing muscle to rehab, as it future-proves you and builds your confidence.

We get more confident the more times we ascend our bank.

Be aware life has a way of pulling us back into the old familiar pattern until we build our self-esteem.

By doing the things you never thought possible, you develop competence so you no longer seek the approval of others or react to their disapproval. Your endorphins give you satisfaction.

Why is it included?

1. Builds momentum: Taking small, manageable steps towards breaking an unhealthy habit can build momentum and create a sense of progress. Each small commitment completed can provide a sense of accomplishment and motivate you to continue towards your goal.

2. Increases confidence: As you make progress and complete bite-size commitments, you will start to build confidence in your ability to break unhealthy habits. This can help you stay motivated and committed to the process.

3. Makes the process less overwhelming: Breaking an unhealthy habit can seem like a daunting task, but taking small, manageable steps can make the process less overwhelming. Breaking the process down into bite-size commitments can make it easier to stay focused and motivated.

4. Increases accountability: By making bite-size commitments, you are setting specific goals and timelines for yourself. This can increase accountability and help you stay on track towards breaking the unhealthy habit.

5. Creates sustainable change: By making small, sustainable changes over time, you are able to create lasting change and maintain healthy habits in the long term.

Example - Story

Simone's Experience

Rock climbing

Explore this practice to gain a deeper understanding:
I have been working with folk that could barely look after themselves when in the tunnel of numbness and doom.

What they still did was

Going to the toilet - even if not often enough, as they forgot to drink water.

They seemed to switch the TV light or heating on fine.

And they usually ate eventually.

These action muscles need to be reconnected at times.

What I suggested in this case was.

Before taking any action, say it out loud.

I am doing... This action (i.e., Switching the tv on) before moving at all.
Saying it three times out loud and then going to do it.

Remember, these are things they would have done without prompting anyhow. Keep it super simple.

Having done this for a few days or as much as a week made them realize they have a choice, and they do things. They are in control.

They might not choose to do certain things, but they are capable of acting on so many.

Questions that might come up in Chapter 9

What if the situation is still the same?
If you are that stuck, this is the time to seek professional help.

What happens out there when I change?

Meeting the situation more grounded and often even physically taller as well as energetically recharged, on top of time having passed, allows the other people involved to also look at the situation from a fresh perspective.

References and Further Reading

1. "Atomic Habits: An Easy & Proven Way to Build Good Habits & Break Bad Ones" by James Clear, published by Avery in 2018.

2. "Mini Habits: Smaller Habits, Bigger Results" by Stephen Guise, published by Selective Entertainment LLC in 2013.

3. "Tiny Habits: The Small Changes That Change Everything" by BJ Fogg, published by Houghton Mifflin Harcourt in 2019.

4. "The Compound Effect: Jumpstart Your Income, Your Life, Your Success" by Darren Hardy, published by Vanguard Press in 2010.

5. "One Small Step Can Change Your Life: The Kaizen Way" by Robert Maurer, published by Workman Publishing Company in 2004.

Sharing with communities

Practical steps into opening conversations in your community

With a struggling individual:

When someone in your community is struggling with managing their distress, it can be challenging to know how to best reach out and offer support. Here are some tips for reaching out:

You are a human interacting with another human – do it with care.

1. **Ground YOURSELF first before reaching out:** This way, your energy is like a life ring already, your voice is calm and smooth, and it demonstrates your confidence and trustworthiness.

2. **Approach with empathy:** Start the conversation by expressing concern for the person's well-being and let them know that you care about them, including their mental health.

3. **Share with tact**: Offer The Empowered Butterfly Method, preferably with an engaging, curiosity-evoking, light conversation (handing them a written summary) or giving a step-by-step demonstration:

Any available mental health resources can be overwhelming due to their complexity. The Empowered

Butterfly Method is simple, and you can lead an individual through a dry run without overstepping boundaries. It's entertaining, to say the least, and will change the energy about being distressed with ease and grace.

4. **Listen actively:** When someone is struggling, it can be helpful to have someone to talk to. Listen actively and without judgment to what they have to say. Show empathy and validate their feelings. Eye contact can be offered but not pushed.

5. **Normalize seeking help**: Let the person know that seeking help is a sign of strength, the first step into a new, better future. That might not even be a clear concept yet, and that is why getting support is so important. At times we can't see the horizon from where we are: we all need a hand up now and again to gain a higher perspective on life.

6. **Follow up:** After you have had a conversation with the person, follow up with them to see how they are doing.

See which steps they remembered and which slipped and if they are open to getting the resources on offer to help them build a new habit. Let them know that you are there for them and that you care about their well-being.

Remember that everyone's mental health journey is unique. It may take time and effort to find the right moment to build trust with someone who is struggling. This is often already there with friends. Be patient and persistent in your efforts to offer support. Encourage them to get appropriate professional help.

"It's not the world
that distresses you
but how you relate to it."

Swami Parthasarathy

-Empowered Butterfly Method-

"It's not the world that distresses you but how you relate to it." -**Swami Parthasarathy**

A: Opening up conversations about mental health with a struggling individual:

When someone in your community is struggling with managing their distress, it can be challenging to know how to best reach out and offer support. Here are some tips for reaching out:

You are a human interacting with another human – do it with care and compassion.

Opening up conversations about mental health in your community is crucial. Help us reach into every corner of the globe:

1. **Let's co-host community events:** Consider co-hosting events together that promote mental health and wellness in your community. These events can provide a safe and inclusive space for individuals to talk about the Empowered Butterfly Method.

2. **Create safe spaces:** Establish safe spaces where individuals can feel comfortable sharing their experiences without fear of judgment or stigma. These could be physical spaces or virtual spaces, such as social media groups or online chat rooms. What is shared remains confidential.

3. **Engage in social media:** Social media can be a powerful tool for starting conversations about the *Empowered Butterfly Method*. Consider connecting, sharing, and adding an invitation to join www.facebook.com/EmpoweredButterflyMethod to your social media. This Facebook site promotes mental health awareness, shares personal stories, and allows us to provide resources and information about the Empowered Butterfly Method.

4. **Help us partner up:** Networking with local organizations brings progress, introducing and matching those trained in *The Empowered Butterfly Method*: Examples are schools, libraries, and

community centers willing to promote mental health awareness.

Be patient and persistent in your efforts to offer support. Encourage them to get appropriate professional help when needed.

Remember, opening up conversations about mental health in your community takes time and effort, but it's a crucial step toward building a safe and supportive environment in which individuals can thrive. By taking practical steps and innovative approaches, we can create a community where mental health is prioritized, and individuals feel safe and empowered to seek help and support when needed.

S.M.I.L.E.
Special Magic In Living Everyday

B: Opening up conversations about mental health in your community is crucial.

Opening up conversations about mental health in your community is crucial. Help us reach into every corner of the globe:

5. **Let's co-host community events:** Consider co-hosting events together that promote mental health and wellness in your community. These events can provide a safe and inclusive space for individuals to talk about the Empowered Butterfly Method.

6. **Create safe spaces:** Establish safe spaces where individuals can feel comfortable sharing their experiences without fear of judgment or stigma. These could be physical spaces or virtual spaces, such as social media groups or online chat rooms. What is shared remains confidential.

7. **Engage in social media:** Social media can be a powerful tool for starting conversations about the *Empowered Butterfly Method*. Consider connecting, sharing, and adding an invitation to join www.facebook.com/EmpoweredButterflyMethod to your social media. This Facebook site promotes mental health awareness, shares personal stories, and allows us to provide resources and information about the Empowered Butterfly Method.

8. **Help us partner up:** Networking with local organizations brings progress, introducing and matching those trained in *The Empowered Butterfly Method*: Examples are schools, libraries, and community centers willing to promote mental health awareness.

9. **We're willing to train community members**: Provide training to community members, such as teachers, coaches, and business owners, on how to identify warning signs of mental health issues and to provide support and resources to those in need.

   Remember, opening up conversations about mental health in your community takes time and effort, but it's a crucial step toward building a safe and supportive environment in which individuals can thrive. By taking practical steps and innovative approaches, we can create a community where mental health is prioritized, and individuals feel safe and empowered to seek help and support when needed.

Help us reach into every corner of the globe:

Let's co-host community events: Consider co-hosting events (in person or online) that promote mental health and wellness in your community. These events can provide a safe and inclusive space for individuals to talk about the Empowered Butterfly Method.

Create safe spaces: Establish safe spaces where individuals can feel comfortable sharing their experiences without fear of judgment or stigma. These can be physical spaces or virtual spaces, such as closed social media groups or online chat rooms. What is shared remains confidential.

Engage in social media: Social media can be a powerful tool for starting conversations about the Empowered Butterfly Method. Consider connecting, sharing, and adding an invitation to join the www.facebook.com/EmpoweredButterflyMethod to your social media that promotes mental health awareness, shares personal stories, and provide resources and information about the Empowered Butterfly Method.

Help us partner up with local organizations by introducing those trained in The Empowered Butterfly Method: Examples are schools, libraries, business organizations, and community centers willing to promote mental health awareness.

We train community members:

We provide online or in-person training to community members, such as mental health professionals, first responders, teachers, coaches, and business owners, on how to identify warning signs of mental health issues and to provide The Empowered Butterfly Method.

Remember, opening up conversations about mental health in your community may take time and effort, but it's a crucial step toward building a safe and supportive environment for individuals to thrive.

By taking practical steps and innovative approaches, we can create a community where mental health is prioritized, and individuals feel safe and empowered to seek help and support when needed.

Know the limits of The Empowered Butterfly Method when you advocate it:

"Help someone in distress
and you lighten your own burden;
the very joy of alleviating
the sorrow of another is the
lessening of one's own."

Fulton J. Sheen

-Empowered Butterfly Method-

"Help someone in distress, and you lighten your own
burden; the very joy of alleviating the sorrow of
another is the lessening of one's own."
- Fulton J. Sheen

One cause of distress lies in how we deal with anxiety as a natural part of our modern, fast-paced culture. It is not always a pathological anxiety that we are dealing with, but more often, a natural one that strengthens our nervous system and aids build myeline sheath to make us more resilient in an ever faster-changing world.

Think of the myelin sheath as the insulation on an electrical wire. Just as insulation helps electrical signals travel more efficiently along a wire, myelin helps nerve impulses travel more efficiently along the nerve fibers in the brain and spinal cord.

Now, imagine that chronic stress and anxiety are like a corrosive substance that eats away at the insulation on the wire. In contrast, levels of well-managed stress can actually promote the growth and development of myelin in the brain.

Studies have shown that when we engage in new activities, we may experience temporary stress as we push ourselves to learn and improve. This stress can trigger the release of growth factors that promote the development of new myelin and strengthen existing myelin in the brain.

The full spectrum of distress:

The attempt
to escape from pain,
is what creates
more pain.

- Gabor Maté

-Empowered Butterfly Method-

The attempt to escape from pain, is what creates more pain. - *Gabor Maté*

Resilience and Emotional Agility
Anxiety is not automatically a disease or disorder.

Stability is needed before you can build resilience, feel the ground under your feet, be in your body, and feel your breath. The '*Empowered Butterfly Method*' is the first step of exactly this and is best learned by being taken through a 'dry run' by someone more familiar with the method. When stuck in survival mode, growth is not the goal; safety is.

Resilience is formed by embracing uncomfortable emotions better and excusing yourself from the situation easier. This is how we create a positive picture of mental health.

Antifragility is a powerful concept introduced by author Nassim Nicolas Taleb in his book, Antifragile: Things That Gain From Disorder[1]. In a nutshell, antifragility means getting stronger in the face of stressors.

Emotional resilience develops similarly to the immune system, which needs to be exposed to bacteria and viruses (stressors) to strengthen. If your Immunity is down, you need to stabilize it before putting yourself into a foreign metropolis eating street food.

Developing an antifragile mindset doesn't mean denying feelings of anxiety and stress, but instead, training ourselves to summon the opposite responses:

With practice, one can combat stress with relaxation, hopelessness with hopefulness, anxiety, and panic with these mindful tools we have carefully crafted into the 'Empowered Butterfly Method.'

This ability to switch perspectives with skill and ease can be seen as the gold standard and can pave the way for training with us to become a member of our team.

Further information on how to train with us is available in the Building Our Team section later.

The '*Empowered Butterfly Method*' fosters:

Resilience
Curiosity
Adaptability/Flexibility
Ability to Trust
Creativity
Reflectiveness
Re-Commitment to a Mission, Values, and Strategy

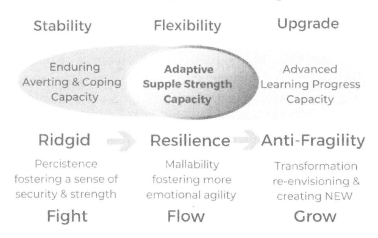

Intensity of change

Stability	Flexibility	Upgrade
Enduring Averting & Coping Capacity	**Adaptive Supple Strength Capacity**	Advanced Learning Progress Capacity
Ridgid	Resilience	Anti-Fragility
Percistence fostering a sense of security & strength	Mallability fostering more emotional agility	Transformation re-envisioning & creating NEW
Fight	Flow	Grow

Anxiety and Excitement

Both cause similar neurological responses in the brain, and the way we label these emotions may be influenced by various factors such as our childhood experiences and cultural background.

Research has shown that anxiety and excitement are both associated with the activation of the sympathetic nervous system, which triggers the release of adrenaline and other stress hormones. This can lead to interchangeable physical sensations such as increased heart rate, sweating, and rapid breathing.

However, the way we interpret and label these sensations can vary. For example, someone who has experienced a lot of distress and trauma in their early life may be more likely to label these physical sensations as threat and anxiety, while someone who has had more positive experiences and role models may be more likely to label them as welcome excitement.

This is not to say that our interpretation of these emotions is entirely determined by our past experiences and cultural background, as cognitive factors such as our beliefs and expectations also play a role.

Overall, it is important to recognize that anxiety and excitement are complex emotions that involve physiological, spiritual, and cognitive processes, and our interpretation of these emotions can be influenced by various factors. By understanding these factors, we can develop more effective strategies for managing our emotions and promoting mental agility leading to better mental health.

There are several external causes of anxiety:

This book will help prepare you to meet those stressors with ease and excitement:

Academic Pressure: Especially young people often feel pressure to perform well academically. Pressure of expectations can come from their parents, peers, or themselves and can lead to anxiety and distress.

Social Media: Social media can create a sense of constant comparison, competition, and pressure to fit in with others. Cyberbullying and online harassment can erode self-esteem, which can lead to anxiety, especially in young people.

Family Conflict: Family conflicts such as parental divorce, domestic violence, financial stress as well as single parenting can lead to anxiety.

Peer Pressure: Peer pressure to fit in or engage in risky behaviors such as drugs, smoking, vaping, and alcohol use can lead to anxiety, especially in young people.

Trauma: Traumatic experiences such as abuse, neglect, or exposure to violence can lead to anxiety.

Uncertainty about the Future: Young people may experience anxiety about their future, such as career or college choices, especially during times of economic uncertainty, more than others.

Health Concerns: Health concerns, either personal or for a loved one, can cause helplessness and anxiety.

Poor attachment in childhood: A lack of secure attachment in childhood lays an eroded foundation, which can lead to mistrust and poor ability to connect socially, contributing to anxiety.

Distress, overwhelm, anxiety, trauma, and beyond

1. **Distress:** Distress refers to a state of discomfort, anxiety, or emotional pain that is usually short-term and can be managed with coping strategies. Distress is a normal part of life and can arise from everyday stressors such as work, school, or relationships.

It is fair to say that The *Empowered Butterfly Method* is the perfect tool for meeting anxiety and distress. This is where the Method is most effective. At this point, a stressed person might be open to reading the book and getting great value and results from the resources themselves.

2. **Overwhelm:** Overwhelm refers to a state of feeling overloaded, either emotionally, cognitively, or physically. It can result from having too much on one's plate or from being faced with a situation that feels too difficult to handle. Overwhelm can be managed by taking breaks, prioritizing tasks, and seeking support.

At this point, we need to take a person by the hand and show the *Empowered Butterfly Method*. Any resistance they will need professional help. You can assist by calling for them

3. **Anxiety:** A natural form of apprehension, tension, or uneasiness that stems from the anticipation of danger, which may be internal or external.

This is different to fear, which is a response to a real threat. Anxiety is a response to a perceived threat when reality does not justify such a response. It is important to remember that the manifestations of anxiety and fear in the body are the same. The big difference with healthy anxiety is you are still in it to win it, and it can be a welcomed heightening of senses.

Fear is an evolutionary essential response to keep us alive. Anxiety has a wide spectrum, from motivating to freezing.

Growth does not happen in your comfort zone. Growth is only possible when not battling with survival. Anxiety is fertilizing hormonal potion when your basic needs are met, and potentially harmful if your needs have not been met.

One of those needs is explained by the attachment theory in childhood. Attachment theory refers to the emotional bond that a child develops with a caregiver, which plays a crucial role in the child's emotional and social development.

Against common belief, Canadian physician and author Gabor Mate CM has discovered that it does not require lots of connections. ONE meaningful trust-based relationship is enough to lay the foundation for feeling a sense of safety in an ever-changing world.

He has a background in family practice and a special interest in childhood development, anxiety disorders, trauma, and the potential lifelong impacts on physical and mental health, including autoimmune diseases, cancer, attention deficit hyperactivity disorder (ADHD), addictions, and a wide range of other conditions.

Anxiety disorder is when one gets stuck in frequent episodes with a small tolerance to change and poor adaptation skills.

It is often too quickly labeled a Pathology rather than teaching missing skills to meet anxiety in a more empowered way. Schools do not aid in meeting this pandemic, causing an increase in the friction points for children. Equipping schools and other social settings with the simple '*Empowered Butterfly Method*' can easily offset the unintended Pathology.

4. Trauma: Trauma refers to a distressing or disturbing event or experience that overwhelms an individual's ability to cope, often resulting in long-term emotional and psychological consequences. Trauma can result from a wide range of events, including physical or sexual assault, natural disasters, accidents, and emotional or psychological abuse. Trauma can lead to symptoms such as flashbacks, nightmares, anxiety, and depression and can have a significant impact on an individual's daily functioning.

5. Complex trauma involves multiple or prolonged traumatic experiences in a relationship context, often during childhood. It can include physical, sexual, or emotional abuse, neglect, abandonment, and exposure to violence. What distinguishes complex trauma is its chronic and repeated nature, leading to long-term and pervasive effects on psychological, emotional, and social functioning. Common examples include childhood abuse, neglect or household dysfunction, exposure to war or community violence, and long-term bullying or harassment. Treatment involves specialized trauma-focused therapy and may require a longer-term approach.

In summary, distress and overwhelm are typically short-term emotional experiences that can be managed with The *Empowered Butterfly Method*.

Trauma and complex trauma refers to a more severe and long-lasting emotional response to one more multiple distressing events or experiences that can have significant and lasting effects on an individual's mental health and well-being. The space for learning something new is so small that, at this point, sharing the *Empowered Butterfly Method* might not meet fertile ground as the ground has been lost for the person experiencing this.

Our vision is to support people before the momentum is so high that turning back without professional help becomes less likely.

Caution to passing on the '*Empowered Butterfly Method*':

The Empowered Butterfly Method aims to reach people before they set foot into the fast-moving river, or at least half a mile before the waterfall and not 50 meters from it when the pull is too great to just lend a hand. Mental health can also affect the helper; it's easy to lose your own footing. Know where a helping hand can make all the difference and know where it can jeopardize your own well-being.

Foundational level training is available to any interested person to manage everyday anxiety and stress, for self-use and supporting family and friends.

In order to become a certified *Empowered Butterfly Method* Practitioner, prior training in the field of mental health is essential. While this simple Empowered Butterfly Method is suitable for all four stages, sensitivity is needed for a more trauma-informed approach.

Contact us for details.

To share the Method, it is important to adopt the K.I.S.S. principle.

Keep It Super Simple.

S.M.I.L.E.
Special Magic In Living
Everyday

Let's build trauma-informed communities

"Help someone in distress
and you lighten your own burden;
the very joy of alleviating
the sorrow of another is the
lessening of one's own."

- Fulton J. Sheen

-Empowered Butterfly Method-

"Let him who expects one class of society to prosper
in the highest degree, while the other is in distress,
try whether one side; of the face can smile while the
other is pinched." - *Thomas Fuller*

Trauma-informed communities are those that recognize and respond to the impact of distress due to trauma on individuals and work to create a safe and supportive environment for those who have experienced trauma.

Here are some basics of trauma-informed communities:

1. **Understanding trauma:** Trauma-informed communities are built on a foundation of understanding how trauma affects individuals and communities. This includes

recognizing that trauma can have lasting effects on a person's physical and mental health, behavior, and relationships.

2. **Safety and trust:** Trauma-informed communities prioritize safety and trust, creating environments where people feel safe to share their experiences and build connections with others.

3. **Equipping the individual with proven and workable tools**: Sharing the *Empowered Butterfly Method* within communities as a way to meet stress and knowing where this tool is not sufficient.

4. Collaboration and empowerment: Trauma-informed communities recognize the importance of collaboration and empowerment. This means working together to support individuals and communities in their healing process and giving them a sense of control over their lives.

5. **Resilience and recovery:** Trauma-informed communities focus on resilience and recovery, recognizing that individuals who have experienced trauma have the potential to heal and grow.

6. Trauma-informed policies and practices: Trauma-informed communities implement trauma-informed policies and practices in all aspects of their work. This includes education, healthcare, criminal justice, and social services.

By creating trauma-informed communities, we can work together to support the healing and growth of individuals and communities affected by trauma.

Building our Team

Building Trust and what does trust truly mean?

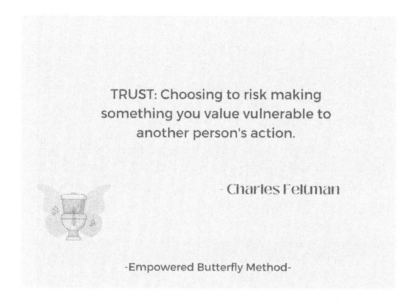

TRUST: Choosing to risk making something you value vulnerable to another person's action.

Charles Feltman

-Empowered Butterfly Method-

This is an introduction to the ethos to consider when building relationships to make a difference in the world of others:

The Thin Book of Trust - 2nd Edition by Charles Feltman is a great basis to build any team, especially in working with the '*Empowered Butterfly Method*' Team.

Trust is a complex concept that is essential for building strong relationships, especially in the work environment.

Vulnerability can take many different forms, ranging from concrete things like money or job security to more intangible things like your beliefs or your sense of happiness and well-being.

When you trust someone, you do so because you believe that their actions will support what you value or, at the very least, will not harm it.

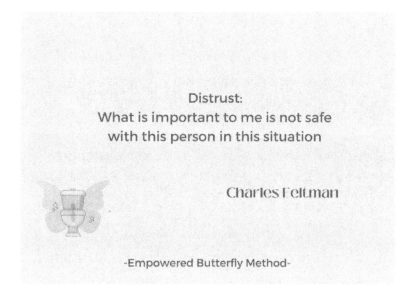

Distrust:
What is important to me is not safe
with this person in this situation

Charles Feltman

-Empowered Butterfly Method-

People tend to approach trust differently.

Some are more trusting and extend trust easily, while others believe that trust must be earned through demonstrated trustworthiness. Much of this has to do with past experiences and your relationship to risk.

Regardless of your personal tendencies, choosing to trust is ultimately a risk assessment.

You assess the probability that the other person will support or harm what you value in the future before deciding to trust or distrust them.

Building and maintaining trust is critical to creating a positive and productive environment. It requires open communication, consistency, and follow-through. If you can't trust, you can't Love.

Looking at it from a different angle, you can only fully trust another person if you trust yourself. The concept of trust gets eroded through adverse childhood experiences (ACEs). The inability to trust can be generations deep.

Planting seeds of trust and allowing them to grow organically vs. expecting them to grow fast or even be there is an often forgotten necessary step in your endeavor to help a struggling person.

The ones able to help are often the ones whose needs were met. Unfortunately, these eager helpers often assume the struggling person's needs were also met and did not realize it's a long-term commitment from planting seeds to seeing growth in sometimes barren soil.

Focusing on building a trusting relationship over fixing a problem for another creates nourishing soil you can easily drop these seeds in and see them grow.

We need community, not just therapists, to create beautiful gardens of hope. This allows for a naturally biodiverse environment for the caterpillar to grow into an empowered butterfly.

The four domains we can assess to rebuild trust, by Charles Feltman

1. Care - you have my back and my best interest in mind

2. Sincerity - speak honestly and act with integrity

3. Reliability - keep specific commitments or be accountable if unable to

4. Competence - you have the experience and skills to do what you say you will.

Underlying this principle is the ability to become **Self-Aware**.

It involves introspection and self-reflection, as well as an awareness of one's own energy levels, strengths, weaknesses, values, and goals.

Be trained and create a hope-filled world

Ultimate vulnerability is a superpower

"We're never more vulnerable
than when we trust someone
but paradoxically,
if we cannot trust,
neither can we find love or joy."

Walter Anderson

-Empowered Butterfly Method-

We're never more vulnerable than when we trust someone - but paradoxically, if we cannot trust, neither can we find love or joy." - **Walter Anderson**

You can easily be trained in the *Empowered Butterfly Method*.

Patricia Kaine, MD, has successfully taught this to patients as part of an office visit.

Groups have easily grasped it due to the all-inclusive logical steps when given a demonstration.

The formula 'see it, do it, teach it' definitely applies to the *Empowered Butterfly Method*.

Be a part of improving the world by connecting others to joy and happiness.

Our Personal Reading List- Book Tips for Personal Development:

"Be as careful of the books you read,
as of the company you keep;
for your habits and character
will be as much influenced
by the former as the latter."

— Paxton Hood

-Empowered Butterfly Method-

"Be as careful of the books you read as of the company you keep; for your habits and character will be as much influenced by the former as the latter."— **Paxton Hood**

To nip Procrastination in the... and to inspire you to inspire others with this simple *Empowered Butterfly Method*

We wish to share a selection of empowering reads that we have found to be beneficial:

Very useful if you are considering making giving others hope part of your life by being trained in the *Empowered Butterfly Method.*

- "The inside track" by Peter Sage
- "Start with WHY" by Simon Simiek
- "Braving the Wilderness: The Quest for True Belonging and the Courage to Stand Alone" by Brené Brown
- "Tiny Habits: The Small Changes That Change Everything" by BJ Fogg
- "The Power of Habit" by Charles Duhigg
- "The Relaxation Response" by Herbert Benson, M.D.
- "Breaking the Habit of Being Yourself" by Dr. Joe Dispenza
- "The One Thing" by Gary Keller and Jay Papasan
- "The Compound Effect" by Darren Hardy
- "The body holds the score" by Dr. Van Der Kolk - 7 steps to get back into the body
- "Innercise: The New Science to Unlock Your Brain's Hidden Power" by John Asseraff

The *Empowered Butterfly Method* draws from a well of Techniques Including but not limited to:

- Guided Imagery & Visualization Techniques
- Metaphorical Stories
- Reframing & Anchoring Techniques
- Subliminal Messaging
- Mindfulness and Breathwork
- Self Acceptance Training
- Cognitive Dissonance Reduction
- Cognitive Priming Techniques

- Cognitive Behavior Therapy
- New Habit Formation Training
- Neural Re-scripting Techniques
- Mental Contrasting Training
- Mindset and Emotional Mastery Training

Epilogue:

"In the Empowerment Triangle, the Creator is the architect of their own destiny, the Challenger is the spark that ignites growth, and the Coach is the compass that guides them along the path of transformation."
Simone Moir

Transforming from distress to hope immensely empowers the individual. This shift aids people in creating healthier relationships with themself and others.

This has been true with The Butterfly Method since its inception. The Divine Being (God, Universe) has known this and desires it for us. More recently, EMPOWERED has been

Incorporated as an acronym in English to make the logical steps of the Butterfly Method easier to remember. As this is translated into other languages, the acronym may not apply, but the underlying concept still applies. People go from the drama triangle Ito the healthier, more fulfilling empowerment triangle, as explained by psychologist David Emerald.

The Acronym EMPOWERED works in English; however, it is tricky to translate.

It's easier to give you a bit of background, so you can too work with it with ease.

Empowered comes from the word POWER which is widely understood.

From Power OVER to power WITH and ultimately power from within each of us.

Stepping out of the hidden triggers

This is a growing process; we can support each other gently. We are bound to trip up, and we can embrace and expect us to fail.

Even momentarily, breaking out of the drama triangle is very useful and needed to make us great coaches, as that will be the most powerful difference you can bring to any situation.

Therapists can often find themselves entangled in the role of rescuer or persecutor.

It involves recognizing one's own role in the dynamic and taking responsibility for one's own actions and emotions.

We are not looking for perfection and are open to inviting new ways of relating with each other.

The Drama Triangle:
We will see it all around us when we become aware of it. Letting go of the need to fix what's broken, rescuing or judging the weaker. It is harder than it seems.

174

The drama triangle is a social model developed by psychologist Stephen Karpman. It consists of three roles: the victim, the persecutor, and the rescuer. These roles can be played by individuals or groups in any type of relationship, including romantic relationships, friendships, families, and workplaces.

The Drama Triangle consists of three roles: Victim, Persecutor, and Rescuer.

The Victim sees themselves as helpless and powerless, often seeking pity and sympathy from others.

The Persecutor is the one who blames and criticizes the victim, often making them feel guilty or ashamed.

The Rescuer is the one who tries to save the victim, often by taking on their problems or offering unsolicited advice.

The drama triangle can create a cycle of dysfunctional behavior and negative emotions, as each role reinforces the other.

There is no movie, no play and no book that ever won an award without this triangle at play. It creates texture and can not be totally avoided. Thats the joy of being a human.

Breaking out of the drama triangle can involve many stages. The following steps especially relevant to the vision of the *Empowered Butterfly Method* team:

Recognizing the roles:

The first step in breaking out of the drama triangle is to recognize the roles that each person is playing. This involves identifying whether you or others are acting as needing help or being short-changed, judging others as better or worse , or feeling the need to help.

Taking responsibility:
Once you recognize your role in the drama triangle, you can take responsibility for your actions and emotions. This means acknowledging your own feelings and needs, and finding healthy ways to express them.

Setting boundaries:
Setting boundaries is important in breaking out of the drama triangle. This means communicating your needs and limits to others and being willing to say "no" when necessary.

Finding healthy support:
Seeking healthy support from friends, family, or a therapist can help you break out of the drama triangle. A supportive person can help you stay accountable and provide a safe space to express your feelings and needs.

By taking these steps, our Empowered Butterfly Method team endeavors to step out of the drama triangle and create healthier, more fulfilling relationships, not just professionally.

Problem-solving can turn into problem-searching if we become fixated on finding problems to solve rather than addressing existing ones. This can be counterproductive and even harmful if we start to create problems where they don't exist or neglect our own needs in the process.

Similarly, helping others can turn into an addiction if we base our self-worth on the amount of good we do for others. This can lead to overcommitment, burnout, and even resentment towards those we are helping. It's important to remember that while helping others can be fulfilling, our self-worth should not be dependent on it.

To avoid these pitfalls, it's important to practice self-awareness and reflection.

The Empowerment Triangle:
This is an alternative social model to the Drama Triangle. Developed by psychologist David Emerald, it seeks to replace the negative and dysfunctional aspects of the Drama Triangle with more positive and constructive roles.

The Empowerment Triangle consists of three roles: Creator, Challenger, and Coach.

Recognizing the opportunities:

We can ask ourselves why we are motivated to solve problems or help others. Are we doing it because it's genuinely helpful, or are we seeking validation or avoiding our own issues? By being honest with ourselves, we can ensure that our actions are truly helpful and not driven by unhealthy motivations.

Additionally, setting healthy boundaries is crucial in both problem-solving and helping. This means being willing to say "no" when necessary and prioritizing our own well-being. It's important to remember that we can't solve all problems or help everyone, and that's okay. By taking care of ourselves, we can ensure that we are in a better position to help others when we are able.

To invite change and growth, it's important to practice self-awareness and reflection.

The Creator is the person who takes ownership of their own life and is proactive in creating the outcomes they desire. They take responsibility for their own feelings, actions, and outcomes, and focus on creating solutions rather than dwelling on problems.

The Challenger is someone who encourages and supports the Creator but also challenges them to grow and develop. They provide honest feedback and hold the Creator accountable for their actions, but do so in a supportive and constructive manner.

The Coach is someone who provides guidance, support, and encouragement to the Creator. They help the Creator identify their strengths and areas for growth and provide tools and resources to help them achieve their goals.

The Empowerment Triangle promotes positive and constructive relationships by focusing on empowerment rather than victimhood. By taking ownership of their own lives, individuals can create the outcomes they desire and build healthier and more fulfilling relationships with others.

Caution Disclaimer:

It is important to note these techniques are not a stand-alone treatment for despair. Breathwork and other self-help techniques, such as mantra repetition, can be helpful for managing symptoms of anxiety, stress, and other mental health conditions, but they are not a substitute for professional medical or psychological treatment. If you are experiencing symptoms of a mental health condition, such as suicidal thoughts or other significant despair, it is important to seek help from a qualified healthcare professional.

It's important to mention that some people may find that certain techniques, like breathwork, may cause them more distress or discomfort. If this is the case for you, discontinue the practice and seek professional guidance.

In summary, it's important to approach any mental health-related self-help technique with care and not use it as a substitute for consulting with a professional. If you have any doubts or concerns about your mental or physical well-being, be wise and contact someone who is trained.

Website

www.EmpoweredButterflyMethod.com

Learn more and download FREE RESOURCES

Discover Additional Empowered tools:
On-The-GO Rescue Card
Mood checker
Bathroom Print and more

How can we help you enrich your community?
Put us in touch with venues open to putting up a sticker in the toilet or businesses, organizations, and places of education that you are involved in and are open to learning and giving more to their communities.

help@EmpoweredButerflyMethod.com

Facebook

www.facebook.com/empoweredbutterflymethod

Help us make a wave. Share, like, and connect. Join the challenge three days - 3 weeks = tools4life. Find an accountability partner - do it as a family or friend.

go-fund-me

YOUR SUPPORT COUNTS

Your money will help us make a meaningful impact.

With YOUR donation, we can create free resources, reach more individuals globally and promote mental well-being through the *Empowered Butterfly Method*.

Join us in making a difference.

Contribute TODAY!

Want to support our upcoming publications, get involved:

THE BUTTERFLY POTTY TRAINING BOOK
THE BUTTERFLY TOILET TRAINING BOOK
SCHOOL MANUAL ELEMENTARY/ PRIMARY
HIGH SCHOOL PACKAGE
INCL MOOD CHECKER APP
COMMUNITY RESOURCES - BRING IT HOME

EMPOWERED
Butterfly Method

Thank you for investing your time in reading, learning, and applying the Empowered Butterfly Method.

We look forward to hearing from you personally.

In awe and wonder about where this movement will take us in our quest to make Suicide the most unappealing option there is.

Patricia and Simone

Printed in Great Britain
by Amazon